Postmarked Yesteryear

ART OF THE HOLIDAY POSTCARD

PAMELA E. APKARIAN-RUSSELL

COLLECTORS PRESS

PORTLAND, OREGON

Library of Congress Cataloging-in-Publication Data

Apkarian-Russell, Pamela.

   Postmarked yesteryear : art of the holiday postcard / by Pamela E. Apkarian-Russell.— 1st American ed.

        p.   cm.

   Includes bibliographical references.

   ISBN 1–888054–54–9 (alk. paper : pbk.)

   1. Postcards—Collectors and collecting.   2. Holidays in art.   3. Postcards—History.   I. Title.

   NC1878.H65 A65 2001

   741.6'83—dc21

                           2001002848

Design: Trina Stahl Design

Editor: Ann Granning Bennett

Printed in China

First American edition

9 8 7 6 5 4 3 2 1

Collectors Press books are available at special discounts for bulk purchases, premiums, and promotions. Special editions, including personalized inserts or covers, and corporate logos, can be printed in quantity for special purposes. For further information contact: Special Sales, Collectors Press, Inc., P.O. Box 230986, Portland, OR 97281. Toll-free: 1-800-423-1848

For a free catalog write to: Collectors Press, Inc., P.O. Box 230986, Portland, OR 97281. Toll-free: 1-800-423-1848 or visit our website at: www.collectorspress.com

Next to the husking bee they went
On happiness and good times bent,
And there the corn in many a sack
Was ready to make into "Cracker Jack."

COPYRIGHT 1907 BY B.E. MORELAND   The "Cracker Jack Bears" Nº 10.

Acknowledgments

I wish to thank the following people for aiding me in researching and writing this book:

Andreas Brown of the Gotham Book Mart, New York, for his help and encouragement. Linda Witherill of Chat Noir, the fairy godmother of all abandoned and homeless cats, for her loan of her Louis Wain cat cards.

The Englishman, Chris Russell, my husband, who has helped me in infinite ways, including keeping Bahron Muhrchoom the Magnificent, our cat, off of the computer when I am using it.

Crystal Snape for being so adept in solving my computer problems.

Jody Young for introducing me to Richard Perry, publisher of this book.

The artists and publishers who for more than a hundred years have had the vision and talent to produce and pass on to us one of our greatest social history documents, the postcard.

TITLE PAGE: NASH-HENDERSON PUBLISHING SET NO. 12

HALLOWEEN CAN TAKE OVER EVEN WHEN IT ISN'T LEAP YEAR. ★★★

OPPOSITE: 1907 THE CRACKER JACK BEARS NO. 10 BY MORELAND.

ONE OF THE MOST POPULAR SETS EVER ISSUED BY A COMPANY TO ADVERTISE THEIR PRODUCT. ★★★

Dedication

This book is for deltiologists everywhere who cherish and wish to perpetuate history and art by preserving postcards. It is for those who study, research, and nourish it. It is for the late Edward Gorey, who collected and created postcards, and for his friend, Andreas Brown of the Gotham Book Mart, who not only is a collector and researcher but who has nurtured many of our collections and has led us on paths we did not know existed. This book is also for those who will discover and explore a world of miniature art and, we hope, will some day add to our knowledge and enjoyment.

To my Valentine

Contents

GERMAN PRINTED CARD WHICH IS PROBABLY BY ARTIST ELLEN CLAPSADDLE. THE COBWEB IS TO CATCH HEARTS IN. ★

A TRUE REFLECTION OF BEAUTY AS, "BEUATY IS IN
THE EYE OF THE BEHOLDER." THE LITTLE GIRL
FEELS THE TURKEY LOOKS QUITE DELECTABLE. ★

Introduction

Deltiology is to postcards what horology is to clocks; a deltiologist is to postcards what a philatelist is to stamps. From the day the first postcard was mailed, people have been fascinated and beguiled by these pieces of paper, these bits of social—and philatelic—history.

There are as many categories of collecting and collectors as there are types of doctors. Just as one physician specializes in cardiovascular disease and another in proctology, a postcard collector might specialize in Christmas or mining. Or that individual could be a generalist who collects a multitude of categories, or someone who collects the views of their hometown or region. The beginning collector can be so overwhelmed by the choices that he or she rushes from one subject to another, just as one would approach a buffet with so much visual and visceral appeal that one must sample each dish.

I have passed up most of the smorgasbord and concentrated on the desserts; in the world of postcard collecting, those are the holiday cards.

I have left out certain holidays, which I would have liked to include, and grouped, for example, all the Patriotics, though they deserve a separate section of their own. Because I am limited by space but wanted to introduce examples from countries that many readers are not familiar with, I chose only the most intriguing. There were hundreds of other cards I wanted to include but sadly had to reject.

My decisions have been difficult, and often the card I chose was of lesser value or not artist-signed, because the symbolism or the motif was one I needed to show. Specific publishers, artists, and types demanded representation or the picture would be incomplete.

Symbolism in art, and in the art of the postcard, is important and is repeated again

STECKER SERIES 408 NO. A

A HIGHLY-EMBOSSED CARD OF A TRICK-OR-TREATER IN A CLOWN COSTUME BEING CHASED BY AN OWL, THE FRIGHT FROM THE NIGHT! ★★★

BULLETS

★ = $10.00 AND UNDER

★★ = $25.00 AND UNDER

★★★ = $50.00 AND UNDER

★★★★ = $100.00 AND UNDER

★★★★★ = $150.00 AND UNDER

★★★★★★ = $200.00 AND UNDER

★★★★★★★ = $300.00 AND UNDER

★★★★★★★★ = $800.00 AND UNDER

and again from one holiday to the next. The similarities as well as the differences in these holidays, both in their imagery and celebration, are an important part of our social history. These cards document the what and how of another time. Historians, architects, and costumers are just a few of the people who turn to postcards to authenticate and date styles and events.

Each holiday has a unique character that evolves with time, and the more you know about that character, the better you will understand and enjoy the holiday. While some holidays are only celebrated in their countries of origin, others are ecumenical; the latter have many faces, while

the other only one. For example, patriotic holidays are observed in most countries. Dates will be different as will bunting colors and events and individuals honored but the day still is a patriotic holiday.

I have tried to show those different aspects by including both holidays and cards representing diverse categories. If at times I investigate the history of postcards and the evolution and symbolism of a holiday rather than the individual card, this is necessary; when you see the cards, whether in this book or in your collection or at a postcard show, you need to recognize and identify the important vistas of holiday-postcard collecting.

Much of the history of postcards has been lost, so we might never discover valuable facts and information. Paper burns whereas clay tablets would have been buried under rubble—a written treasure to be found by archeologists centuries later. World War II destroyed more than people's lives; it annihilated part of our global heritage. For example, the fire-bombing of Dresden, Germany, destroyed all records of printers, publishers, and manufacturers. A bomb hit London's Tuck Publishing during that same war, wiping out most of their records. On January 12, 1910, Whitney Publishing burned to the ground, snuffing out its inventory, as well as the records of the companies it bought and absorbed—

including Esther Howland, the most important name in American valentines. Because dedicated deltiologists have spent uncountable amounts of time making checklists and tracking data from other sources, we have information that was not available even a few years ago. Postcard collectors owe these researchers much gratitude. They and others who follow will continue to add to our knowledge and enjoyment.

We can make comparisons, assemble checklists, compare art styles, and attribute certain cards to particular countries, and that is a step in the right direction. However, chances are we will never know the identity of the artists who designed or illustrated the cards. We probably will never know the number of cards produced and distributed, or to what stores, or the names of the lithographers, engravers, photographers, and models for many of the cards we cherish.

Publishers often did not allow artists to sign their work, as they would then be "named" artists, develop a following, and demand more money. But deltiologists continue to pursue the search. Often the way an image is depicted and the symbols used can help us attribute a card to a specific country or artist. A piece of ephemera, such as a bill or letter, might provide the clue that pinpoints a publisher or an artist. The artist HB Griggs, for example, was prolific, but no

TUCK #6054

A&G TAYLOR'S "ORTHOCHROM" BY ARTIST H. WAITE SHOWS A VERY PROGRESSIVE SANTA FLYING OVER LONDON. THIS IS A VERY UNUSUAL RENDITION AND IT ACTED AS A HERALD INTO THE MODERN AGE. ★★★

one knows if Griggs was a man or a woman or what the HB stands for. If a letter to Leubrie and Elkus Publishing of New York existed and was signed by Griggs, we might be able to determine Griggs's gender and perhaps the compensation he or she received for the work. On the rare occasion if we find the original artwork, we might be able to identify an artist.

A deltiologist is much like a detective: we must find clues in order to solve the crime. Little by little, we find a clue here and another one there. But the jigsaw puzzle is so vast and complicated that the average collector throws up his hands and says, "It's not all that important to me. Let some-

A merry Christmas.

one else worry about it." In the end, all information can do is enhance your knowledge of your hobby; the cards and the art stand by themselves.

Our ability to understand holidays and their symbolism varies with the depth of our knowledge. If one sees a picture postcard of the nativity but has never heard of Christmas, all one sees is a man, a woman, and a baby in a stable with a bright star overhead. They are just three people in a manger. They have no meaning for us. But we might get a clue if a message were written on the back in a language we could read, incorporated into the decor of the card, or on the front, such as "Buon Natale" or "Merry Christmas," that is easily understood.

Another example of how our culture has molded our recognition is the figure of the Gift Giver. Is he Father Christmas with twinkling eyes and kindly face, the old gentleman in flowing robes who walks house to house through the snow bringing fruits and toys to well-behaved children? Is this the friend of animals and angels, similar in looks and bearing to the wizard Gandalf in Tolkien's *Lord of the Rings*? Or is this Saint Nicholas more like a stern bishop carrying a

CIRCA 1909 FATHER CHRISTMAS IN A BLUE SUIT TRIMMED WITH BROWN FUR, OPENING HIS SACK OF TOYS TO A LITTLE BOY AND GIRL. ★★★

staff and wearing a miter? Or could this be Thomas Nast's Santa Claus, a jolly fat man, flying through the air, a jolly old elf in his red BVDs? Or is he Father Frost, the Gift Giver of Russian folklore?

Obviously, cultures depict the Gift Giver differently. Even the Magi, the Three Wise Men, bearing gold, myrrh, and frankincense to the Christ child were enacting a much older tradition.

When postcards first were sent the ancient roots of religions had been incorporated into the new. Through postcards we can see ancient symbols that have become icons of our culture and religions, and we can investigate their origins. We will look at only a few of the symbols. Perhaps they will whet your appetite and help you appreciate this art, still so vibrant and unique that it is reproduced by greeting card companies and shown in museums.

Certainly value is subjective. Some cards are beautiful, but because they attract few collectors, they are undervalued. This means they are easy to acquire and can be purchased reasonably. Other cards, such as those by Louis Wain and Samuel Schmucker, are in great demand and command premium prices.

Many collectors are frustrated in their search because the cards they seek were not distributed in their home country. For example, Halloween cards were produced only for the American market, but many British collectors hunger for cards by Tuck Publishing and artist Francis Brundage's cats and owls. For them, these cards cost more because they usually must be purchased in the United States. On the other hand, many artists' works were only produced for

GIBSON SERIES 120, FROM A SET OF
TWELVE BY FRANCES BRUNDAGE.
BRUNDAGE'S ROSY-CHEEKED CHILDREN AND
SQUEEZABLE KITTENS ARE THE ESSENCE OF
HALLOWEEN INNOCENCE. ★★★ EACH

England or Europe and are difficult to find and costly for American and Canadian collectors. If the collector has access to the Internet, he or she can track down some of the cards by favorite artists or those commemorating a treasured holiday. The rarer cards are more difficult to obtain and it is not unknown for collectors to spend decades, travel thousands of miles, and look at millions of cards without completing a set or locating that most wanted card.

I have provided a guide to what I believe the cards are worth. Some I feel should sell for more, and others I feel are overvalued on today's market. Over my thirty years of international trading, I have seen great differences in prices worldwide, and even venue to venue and dealer to dealer. I have tried to strike a happy medium but with Internet auctions and fluctuations that remind one of the commodities market, it is difficult to predict what a card will bring.

Condition is always important to desirability—and price. Never pass up a scarce card because the condition is not mint. You many never find it again. Use common sense. Never buy for investment. These cards are works of art. Collect only what you love, and disregard possible future returns. We have seen prices on certain cards decrease because a category has been priced out of reach to the collecting public, therefore lessening the demand. But prices

increase because so many have found the beauty and joy of collecting them.

Display your cards and enjoy them. Keep them in acid-free pages in albums. Frame them and place them on walls just as you would a painting. You can even put them in hard plastic sleeves, attach a hanger to the back, and use them to decorate an artificial tree. Some collectors keep a Christmas tree up year round, changing the cards for each new holiday. One collector of hold-to-light cards has created mobiles in order to see the illuminations at a full advantage. Postcards are an adventure you can enjoy every day and their beauty will enhance yours and others' lives.

LITTLE GIRL WITH HYACINTH. A LOVELY CARD,

BUT WITHOUT THE BORDER AND THE WORDING IT

COULD BE AN EASTER CARD! ★

Easter Greetings.

GERMAN PRINTED NO. 349.

THIS LOOKS MORE LIKE GANG WARFARE THAN AN EASTER GREETING. TWO SPECIES, THE FROGS AND BEES, ATTACK THE RABBITS. INTERSPECIES RELATIONS WAY BACK THEN WERE AS BAD AS INTERNATIONAL RELATIONS ARE TODAY. THIS IS AN UNUSUAL IMAGE FOR A HOLIDAY, WHICH IS SUPPOSED TO BE ONE OF HOPE AND PEACE. ★★

THE TRANSCONTINENTAL train, the automobile, and the airplane each increased the speed of communication by mail during the past century. Now, all you need is to do is jump on the Internet, type a greeting, and within minutes your family and friends will have received your message.

A secondary effect of the Internet is

Significant dates in the history of postcards

that you can initiate a search, and within an hour or two purchase an Easter postcard from a dealer in Romania or Germany. Our ability to locate and buy is now global in nature.

Postcard collections grew long ago because it was possible for a lady in Maine to buy several copies of a Fourth of July card and send one to a postcard pal in California, another to Texas, and a third to Richmond, Surrey, U.K. Those friends in turn would send cards available in their areas. Whether it was greetings or views, the trading craze was almost as important as owning or receiving the cards.

Often, we turn over a card and read a note saying that the card is for the recipient's collection or thanking the sender for the card. These collections are why so many cards survived even after sitting dormant for decades. It is also why so many collections are more like accumulations and range from beautiful cards to some that aren't worth a cent. Here are some highlights.

1843. Charles Dickens's *A Christmas Carol* is published. John Calcott Horsley designs, lithographs, and hand-colors the first Christmas card for Sir Henry Cole. The illustration showed a wealthy family enjoying Christmas dinner and toasting the

card's recipient. On the side are vignettes of the less fortunate. The card bears the inscription "Merry Christmas and a Happy New Year." Only 1,000 of these were made. These had blank backs and are considered the mother of the postal greeting card.

Jan 10, 1840. England's Royal Mail establishes uniform penny postage.

1869. The Correspondez-Karte, the world's first postcard, is introduced in Austria.

1870. The Royal Mail issues its first postcards in two sizes. Eventually, the larger of the two was discontinued, as it was ungainly and difficult to handle without damaging. Queen Victoria is pictured on this half-penny government postal.

October 1, 1870. Léon Besnardeau makes picture postcards for the troops stationed near his village of Sille-le-Guillaume, France. This inventor of the picture postcard waited twenty years for them to be issued. The Swiss and British governments introduce their official postcards. In the U.K., they are issued with an imprinted violet-colored stamp that coincidentally is the first day of issue for the stamp. They cost a halfpenny and are instantly a hit with the general public. They are not as welcomed by stationers, as they are unable to sell cards on which postage is printed. Two years pass before stationers received a partial concession from the Royal Mail, stating that selling the stamp and giving away the postal stationery is taking unfair advantage of the entrepreneur.

June 1871. Canada issues its first postcard.

1872. Russia issues its first postcard. In June, the use of private mailing cards is approved, and in July, Germany follows suit.

1874. By this year, France, Chile, Romania, most of the Scandinavian countries, Italy, and Japan all produce official postcards.

1875. In September, an international conference meets in Bern, Switzerland, and the General Postal Union is formed. Four years later, this conference meets in Paris and becomes the General Postal Union (GPU).

1889. Construction begins on the Eiffel Tower, infuriating some Parisians who call it a "barbarous mass," looming over the

SERIES 3241 MEISSNER & BUCH, CIRCA 1937. "WE'LL RAISE A CUP OF KINDNESS YET FOR AULD LANG SEIN." MIDNIGHT IS THE TIME TO CELEBRATE. ★★

SIGNED JENNY NYSTRÖM. THREE WONDERFUL
EASTER WITCHES FLYING OFF TO BRING SOME
LUCK, HAPPINESS, AND PROSPERITY TO
A HOME. ★★

skyline. But when it opens in May as part of the Exposition Universelle, it is the most visited attraction and becomes the grand symbol of the City of Lights. In celebration of the event, the picture side of the postcard shows the 318.7-meter high landmark.

The 1890s. The birth of the Gruss Aus card in Germany, the Souvenir in France, and Ricordi de in Italy. These early greeting post cards show lithographs, the predecessor of the pictorial greeting card. The earliest ones are printed in only one color. But with the advent of chromolithography, four-color reproductions become immensely popular.

1893–1898. The Pioneer Era of postcards. On May 1, 1893, the U.S. Government postal cards as well as privately printed cards showing scenes from the World's Columbian Exposition in Chicago are issued. The address side of the card was not for writing messages as they are today. When you wanted to write a greeting, you wrote it over or beneath the picture. The U.S. Government imprinted a one-cent stamp; the sender had to affix an additional two-cent stamp.

1894. George Stuart of Edinburgh, Scotland, produces the first privately printed half-penny cards. On the message side, they show small views of—where else—Edinburgh.

1895. James Valentine & Sons, of Dundee, Scotland, using the Collotype method of printing, begins printing views of many places. When Queen Victoria celebrates her Diamond Jubilee in 1897, the craze for collecting picture postcards forges ahead like a runaway steam engine.

1898–1901. The Era of the Private Mailing Card. On May 19, 1898, an act by the U.S. Congress allows private printers to produce and sell cards that require a one-cent stick-on stamp. Most publishers provide a small white border at the bottom of the picture side to allow the sender to write a short message.

1899. In The Court Card made its appearance in England. The size regulations were altered from 115mm x 89mm, and the standard 5½" x 3½" became the norm. This gives publishers more room to work. On November 1, 1899, Tuck is the first British publisher to sell the new full-sized card—which seems only fair as his firm played a major role in lobbying for this reform. The card is a lovely chromo-lithographed card of the Tower of London with boats on the Thames. There was also the image of a Beefeater in the lower right corner. Forty-seven more cards followed as part of this first set.

By this time, Tuck Publishing was a well-respected stationer and held a Royal Warrant. Even Queen Victoria was a passionate postcard collector. She adored accumulating pictures of herself, her extended family throughout the world, famous people, and colorful scenes. The British naturally followed their monarch's lead in sending and collecting postcards—a pastime that already had captivated most of Europe. Sadly, the Queen passed away before the Golden Age of postcards; she would have been one of its greatest patrons.

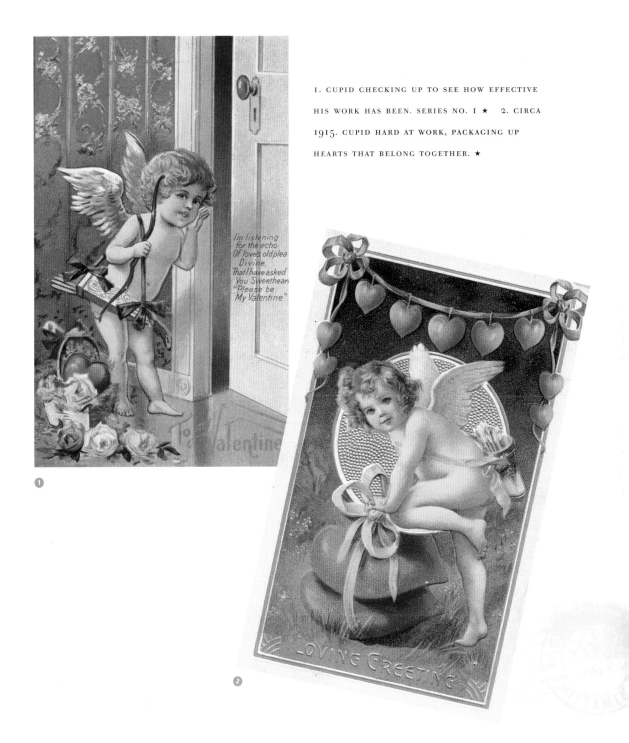

1. CUPID CHECKING UP TO SEE HOW EFFECTIVE HIS WORK HAS BEEN. SERIES NO. 1 ★ 2. CIRCA 1915. CUPID HARD AT WORK, PACKAGING UP HEARTS THAT BELONG TOGETHER. ★

A Happy New Year

1898. A set of thirty-five poster cards is published in France, including signed cards by Alphonse Maria Mucha and Henri de Toulouse-Lautrec. A complete set today would cost a pretty penny as they represent the best known artists of the period, as well as some of the greatest classics in poster art.

1899. Cards from Germany depicting the Boer War, showing men in military uniforms and emblazed with anti-British propaganda, are so colorful and well-executed that even the British seek out these cards.

1900. In China, the military attack foreign embassies and kill missionaries and Christian converts. Called the Boxer Rebellion, it was a nationalist movement and considered by many of the Chinese a patriotic movement. The harsh, anti-Chinese cartoon cards that follow the Boxer Rebellion are mild in comparison to later ones of protest.

1904–1905. The Russo-Japanese War produces some horrific cartoon cards, as well as portraits of the participants at the peace negotiations. These include President Teddy Roosevelt, who enjoyed seeing depictions of himself. During the peace negotiations in Portsmouth, New Hampshire, bro-

A MOST CHARMING RENDITION OF AN ELF KISSING A SUNFLOWER. ★★★★

kered by Roosevelt, the Russians who had lost on the battlefield won back everything at the negotiation table. A wealth of these cards exists.

1901–1907. An act of the U.S. Congress on December 4, 1901, allows private citizens to take photographs and have them printed with postcard backs. Some hand-drawn ones are also produced with postcard backs. Messages are required to be placed on the front or picture side.

1893–1907. The Era of Undivided Backs. This means that the vertical rule that often appears on contemporary postcards, dividing the message from the address, did not exist.

July 1900. The first publication to be dedicated to postcards is distributed. *The Picture Postcard Magazine* was published until 1907 by E.W. Richardson.

1907–1914. On March 1, 1907, the U.S. Postal Service allows a vertical rule to be printed on the back of the postcard, dividing the left-hand message side from the right-hand address side. The front of the card was reserved for an unblemished image. Great Britain had adopted this measure in 1902. By 1907, this configuration is permissible almost everywhere.

1914–1918. World War I is fought in Europe. Germany was the source of much of the best printing and lithography. Lithography, a process in which a series of engraved stones print layer upon layer of color on paper on pasteboard, which had been used for many years in the United States, England, and Germany. Because this process was less expensive and better executed in Germany, many cards sold in England and the U.S. were printed there. Even Tuck, the pre-eminent name in English cards, sent some of its work to Germany for reproduction. When war broke out, this all stopped.

1914. Whitney Made of Worcester, Massachusetts, places its distinctive red "W" logo on the back of its cards.

1915–1930. Cards depicting picturesque scenes bear a white border and are called White Border Cards. To match the low cost of German-printed cards, printers try to skimp on production materials. If the card was to "bleed" on all sides, that is, cover the entire postcard surface, the printer had to print beyond that edge, then trim to the correct size, thus using more paper. Creating a white border allows him to save a bit of paper and ink. Furthermore, the industry fails to pay living wages to experienced craftsmen; instead, they hire unskilled

CIRCA 1915, RUSSIAN CHRISTMAS FORTUNE TELLING CARDS BY
GRAPHIC ARTIST S. LLOCHINSKI. BORN IN 1917, THIS ARTIST
DID SIXTY CARDS OF RUSSIAN SUBJECTS AND GREETINGS.
REGARDLESS OF THE ETHNIC CULTURE, THE AGE OLD CUSTOMS
PREDOMINATE THE HOLIDAY AND CHRISTMAS WAS AS GOOD A
TIME AS ANY TO PEEK INTO THE FUTURE AND SEE IF THERE
WAS A TRUE LOVE COMING ONES WAY. ★★ EACH

labor. Consequently, mistakes and misprints frequently appear on cards of this era. The cards' poor quality make avid collectors, as well as the general public, lose interest. Citing high labor costs, many of these printers went out of business.

1915–24. Global instability does not cease with the peace treaties of World War I. The thousands of postcards brought home by the soldiers showing consequent devastation do not deter some countries from perpetrating atrocities. Postcards of the Starving Armenians, targets of the first genocide of the 20th century, incense the British, French, and Americans. Their governments, however, do nothing to stop a million and a half people from being destroyed. This is the first time a tragic event was captured in photographs and widely circulated via the postcard.

1930–1944. Paper mills begin to process cotton rags in combination with wood pulp in the manufacture of paper. This allows the manufacturer to apply a rich, textured-linen finish to the sheet, giving these cards their name, Linens. Many printing companies spring up to take the place of those that had gone under, and some of them become quite successful. With the rapidly changing technology, people are more mobile than in the past. Not only the wealthy are traveling. The working classes are hopping on trolleys

and trains and—even better—into the automobile. Travelers send remembrances in the form of postcards to show places visited and sights seen. The cards are vibrant and colorful in a completely different way than the holiday cards. Cards produced for the 1939 New York World's Fair are perhaps the apex of these stylized cards. Collectors who like Art Deco and Deco revivals are attracted to these cards because of their style and color. While some turn their noses up at Linens, they are missing some of the more interesting cards produced in the United States. The advertising cards of this period document its economic and social history.

1945–present. Union Oil Company produced views to sell in its gasoline stations. These cards were called Photochrome cards after the process of producing them. But collectors refer to them as Chromes.

The 3-D card also was produced during this era. It was a novelty that had a short but memorable run. They might be garish, especially the moving ones, but they are great to look at. Disney produced many of these, and occasionally we see a holographic image on a book, a U.S. postal envelope, or cover of *National Geographic.* Their depth and vibrancy are visually exciting.

I have offered but a few highlights of postcard history. Details I have left out could easily fill many a book.

TUCK SERIES 807 BY ARTIST GRACE WEIDERSHIMER DRAYTON, ORIGINATOR OF THE CAMPBELL SOUP KIDS. ★★★★★★

Postcard Artists and Publishers

SIGNED BY AURELIO BERTIGLIA. ★★★

THIS BOOK's bibliography is a good starting point for researching post-card artists and publishers. Another source for learning is the postcard show. The smaller fairs provide the chance to spend time with dealers—particularly on the second day, when the atmosphere is less intense and the dealers are less rushed. Other collectors you meet often are pleased to give the novice a helping hand.

Dealers file cards under a variety of categories. Usually, they place cards where they feel they will sell the quickest—and not necessarily where a collector would think to look. Depending on the size and quality of a dealer's inventory, he might have special sections for certain types of cards. For instance, he might have a large group of cat cards but no Louis Wain cards. Or, he might have a special section for Louis Wain. Each vendor's stock is as different as his clientele. A well-placed question will cut down your looking time.

Collectors find antique and collectible shows provide good hunting grounds for postcards. Other sources are antique stores and specialty postcard dealer shops, where cardophiles can find boxes of tempting wares.

Artists

Francis Lockwood Brundage

Francis Lockwood married the marine artist William Brundage. Her earlier works were for Tuck. Today, these are more in demand than those she did for Sam Gabriel Publishing because those she did for Tuck are more colorful and better crafted. Not only did she illustrate postcards, she provided drawings for children's books, calendars, and prints. Her children are rosy-cheeked and well-loved. She signed much of her work, but some cards by her only bear a faint set of initials. Brundage did a few cards in partnership with her husband. She died in 1937 at age 83.

Ellen Clapsaddle

Clapsaddle was the most prolific of all the American postcard artist. She worked for the American company International Art Publishing which later was purchased by Wolf Publishing. Her cards for International Art were usually embossed; the harder-to-find Wolf cards are not. Because of the high prices and shortages of paper and ink caused by World War I, Wolf went out of business. Clapsaddle found herself stranded in Germany but a Wolf attorney arranged for her passage back to America.

Although she never married, Clapsaddle is known for her sensitive drawings of children. She also produced cards depicting flowers and many honoring various holidays. As a matter of fact, her illustrations of women are superior in quality to those of her children, though not as desirable.

Clapsaddle, who died in 1934 at age 69, was not a great artist; however, she occupies an important position in postcard history because she covered such a broad spectrum of subjects and because her children are such accurate reflections of the time. They are as avidly collected today as they were at the height of her popularity—in particular, her Halloween and mechanicals with their moving parts.

Grace Drayton

Grace (Gebbie) Weidersheim (first husband) Drayton (second husband) is the Mother

TUCK'S SANTA CLAUS SERIES NO. 512. A BEAUTIFUL CHILD, POSSIBLY RENDERED BY ARTIST FRANCIS BRUNDAGE, IS DELIVERING GIFTS. ★

With Love's Greeting.

of the Campbell Kids. Even before they became the marketing symbol of the Campbell Soup Company, these rosy-cheeked, fat-legged children were popular characters. The Campbell Kids showed up on two sets of postcards and similar looking children appeared on many more of Drayton's postcards. Drayton wrote and illustrated books, designed paper dolls, and illustrated magazines. Her Dolly Dingel cutouts were a sensation with children whose mothers read *The Ladies Home Journal,* and she de-signed a few sets of advertising cards for Campbell that are highly desirable. Her sister, M.G. Hayes, also designed postcards, but she did not attain the popularity of her sibling. Today, Drayton is almost forgotten—few could identify her as the inventor of the Campbell Kids, but people recognize her art. She died on January 31, 1936, in New York at age 59.

HB Griggs

To this day, we do not know Griggs's gender or what his or her initials stand for. He— or she—adds to our confusion by sometimes

INTERNATIONAL ART CO. EMBOSSED FAIRIES AMIDST THE MORNING GLORIES. UNSIGNED BUT PROBABLY THE WORK OF ELLEN CLAPSADDLE, WHO WAS THEIR MOST PROLIFIC AND IMPORTANT ARTIST. ★★

signing in fancy lettering "HBG" rather than "HB Griggs." Vivid colors mark his work, which is almost cartoon-like in style. Lubrie and Elkins Publishing of New York published most of Grigg's pieces. Although the content often borders on the political, Griggs's zany approach has lasting appeal to postcard collectors.

Raphael Kirchner

A graduate of Vienna's Akademie der Bildenden Kunste, he began his career as a portrait painter of elegant, bourgeois women. Soon he became celebrated for his renderings of saucy wenches, and his work was in demand for books, sheet-music covers, magazines, and postcards, not only in Austria but also in Germany, France, England, and America. Periodicals often featured his women in full color; they might have been goddess-like in demeanor, but they still displayed a sense of humor. Decades later, illustrator Varga (née Vargas) drew on Kirchner for inspiration. Kirchner's early works command high prices. He died in New York at age 41.

Jenny & Curt Nyström

Jenny Nyström is the first name in cards from Sweden. Nyström studied art in Paris then returned home and began illustrating for Axel Eliasson Art Publishing Company in Stock-holm. Some of her first paintings

for him were of Tomtar, the Swedish version of Santa Claus. (In 1931, when The Coca-Cola Company asked illustrator Haddon Sund-blom to create a Santa Claus for its promotional material, he turned to the work of his fellow Swede—Nyström—for inspiration.) She went on to become a premier artist, creating ethnic folk symbols such as elves with bright scarlet hats and witches with benevolent expressions. Her son Curt eventually followed in her footsteps. Nyström's cards developed a devoted following in the Scandinavian countries and beyond. Nyström died in 1946 at the age of 89.

LUBRIE & ELKINS (L&E) PUBLISHING SERIES 2230 SIGNED BY ARTIST HBG (GRIGGS) SHAMROCKS AND FANCY SCRIPT ADD TO THE UNMISTAKABLE WORK OF A PROLIFIC ARTIST. ★★

R.F. Outcault

Richard Fenton Outcault originated the Yellow Kid and Buster Brown. His cards are highly desirable because some are now more than a century old. For many years, Outcault's work appeared in Sunday supplements as a full-page comic strip. Later, his postcards were included in the supplement; readers could cut them out and save them. His Buster Brown calendar advertising cards are popular. Because some holiday card collectors only want the month represented by their holiday-of-choice, finding a complete set is difficult. October cards usually cost a bit more than others. Outcault died in 1928 at age 65.

Samuel Schmucker and John Winsch Publishing

John Winsch Publishing of New York contracted with two significant artists, Jason Freixsas and Samuel Schmucker. Of the two, Schmucker is the more important. Born on February 20, 1879, he attended the Pennsylvania Academy of Fine Arts. Though he produced much of his work for Winsch, he also drew cards for Tuck, Detroit, and Whitney Made Publishing. His stunning women and Art Nouveau style with intricate backgrounds make his work the highest priced of American postcard artists. He died at age 42 in 1929.

RAPHAEL KIRCHNER WAS THE PREDECESSOR OF VARGAS. HIS SAUCY NAKED AND SEMI-NAKED WOMEN WERE PURE AND INNOCENT AS WELL AS SEXY AND ALLURING. THEIR PERFECT BODIES, CONFORMING TO THE TASTE OF THE TIMES, ARE AN OXYMORON OF SEDUCTIVE AND UNTOUCHABLE. THE MISTLETOE IS JUST A COME-ON FOR A FANTASY, A DAYDREAM. ★★★★★ EACH

Alfred Schonian

Alf, as he signed his cards, was born in Germany in 1856. Little is known about this master of still life and animals. His horses and dogs are popular with collectors, and his dwarves stand up well with those of artist Heinrich Schlitt, designer of many

valuable beer steins. Shonian's attention to detail and use of dark backgrounds make the colors on the main image stand out, lending a hauntingly realistic look to a fantasy subject.

Louis Wain

Louis Wain is the father of the anthropomorphic cat. He dressed his subjects as humans and placed them in real-life situations. So popular did they become that they appeared by the thousands in books, magazines, and anthologies and—to our delight—on postcards, attracting an international following that carries on to this day.

Born on August 6, 1860, in London, his artistic talent as a child led him to the classrooms of the West London School of Art in 1877. After three years of study, he stayed on as an assistant master for two more years.

Upon his father's death, he became the sole support of his mother, five sisters, and wife Emily, ten years his senior. In an attempt to become financially stable, he began to freelance. Having adopted Peter, a black-and-white kitten, he was attracted to cat shows, and some time later his famous "A Kitten's Christmas Party" appeared in the *London News* Christmas edition.

Sadly, Emily developed an incurable disease and died in 1887, when Wain was twenty-six years old. Four years later he became president of the National Cat Club, an office he held until 1907. Living once more with his family, Wain began to find recognition and financial success in illustrating books and postcards.

By the advent of the new century, Wain had become a household name. His Louis Wain Cat was a mischievous feline with a cocky attitude and a penchant for fancy dress. He appeared even on china and a talcum powder tin.

After Wain's eldest sister died in 1917, people began questioning his mental state—although he surely had been an eccentric for many years. Meanwhile, Wain continued to depict cats, even though the popularity of his output took a downward turn. Finally, he was diagnosed as schizophrenic and certified insane on June 16, 1924. He was admitted in poverty to a mental hospital. Even in the institution, he remained quite active in producing wonderful paintings and sketches.

There, many years later, a doctor recognized him and wrote a letter to a friend about his plight. People who loved his work rallied and responded with money donations, allowing him to spend his final years in relative comfort. He died at age 89.

Wain's work remains extremely sought-after. His human-like and loveable felines continue to amuse and fascinate. Wain also has been of interest to researchers of schizophrenia. Because he concentrated on one subject and because so much of his work is available for review, students are able to trace the progression of his mental illness.

Bernhardt Wall

With wide-eyed children as his trademark, Wall is best known for his series of Sunbonnet Babies. After the Spanish-American War, he worked for Ullman Publishing Company which published many of his cards. Wall's black-and-white cards are far less dramatic than his vividly colored ones enhanced with gold. Also desirable are his Halloween sets, depicting highly-gilded veggie people; these are difficult to find in

good condition, especially ones with a delicate gelatin finish that tend to peel. On the other hand, Wall's Dutch children with their almost nauseating baby talk are dated and haven't much of a following. All in all, his cards vary in value depending on the publisher and the topic. He died in 1956 at age 84.

Publishers

Curteich Publishing

Widely known for its Linen-Era postcards, Curteich was a major producer of view cards. Collectors of Art Deco especially appreciate the style as expressed in distinctive

SIGNED LOUIS WAIN, SANTA DELIVERING MICE AND OTHER THINGS KITTENS WOULD THINK AS NICE. MOST FELINE LOVERS WOULD FIND THIS SANTA MORE LOVABLE AND MORE BELIEVABLE THAN THE JOLLY FAT MAN. ★★★★★★★

2188

ULLMAN SERIES 115 NO. 2188

SIGNED BY ARTIST BERNHARDT WALL SHOWS A
CLAY PIPE SMOKING FROG DRESSED IN A TOP HAT
AND CARRYING A SHALLEGHLY IN ONE HAND AND
THE FLAG OF IRELAND IN THE OTHER. BECAUSE HE
IS GREEN HE PROBABLY FEELS THAT THIS IS A
HOLIDAY HE CAN REALLY LEAP INTO. ★★

colors. Curteich has organized an exhibit—Bringing the World Home—currently on display at the Lake County Discovery Museum, showcasing not only its products but also those of other manufacturers. For those interested in broadening their knowledge of this field, this is the place to go.

Address: Lakewood Forest Preserve, Rt. 176 and Fairfield Road, Wauconda, Ill. 847-968-3400. *www.co.lake.il.us/forest/educate.htm*

The George C. Whitney Company

Born on September 18, 1842, George Whitney left school to fight in the Civil War with the 51st Regiment of Massachusetts Volunteers.

In 1858, Whitney's brother Sumner opened a wholesale stationery store in Worcester, Massachusetts, at 218 Main Street. A second brother, Edward, became a partner the following year and took over management after the death of Sumner. George joined the company in 1863 after receiving an honorable discharge. The brothers worked together at the Whitney Valentine Company until 1869, the year Edward resigned.

By 1888, George Whitney had bought out ten major valentine producers, including Esther Howland's and Edward Taft's New England Valentine Company and Jothan Taft's Grafton firm. He acquired equipment, allowing him to produced embossed papers,

full-color ornaments, and printed verses. Whitney's Valentines bore the distinctive red "W" on the card's back. Soon, he added postcards to his prolific offerings. Whitney's artistic quality varied; some cards were mundane and others, such as those picturing children, were wonderful—and extremely collectible. Nimble Nicks, for example, were a Whitney creation. Whitney hired talented artists, but none signed their work. (We have been able to identify Fern Bissel Peat as an illustrator of Halloween cards.)

On January 12, 1910, a fire destroyed the Whitney plant. Reduced to ash were $200,000 worth of stock and $100,000 worth of printing equipment. Fortunately, Whitney had just shipped his Valentines to stores throughout the country. Using insurance money, he purchased a building at 67 Union Street in Worcester, Massachusettes.

When George Whitney died in 1915, his son Warren took over. By the 1930s, the delicate, hand-applied slivers of paper and lace had proved too expensive and were replaced by mass-produced valentines marked on the backs "Whitney Made/ Worcester, Mass."

The firm continued in business until February 27, 1942, only a few months short of the one hundredth anniversary of George Whitney's birth. The reason for closing was paper shortages caused by World War II.

Gibson Art Company

Gibson opened for business in Cincinnati, Ohio, and produced many cards over the years. However, critics call its graphics "often mediocre." Often, cards were printed in one color, then hand-colored. Among the better-known artists working for Gibson were Bernhardt Wall, Rose O'Neill (creator of the Kewpies), and Kathleen Elliot. Verses appearing on Gibson cards were somewhat mundane, but in their own way rather delightful. Gibson did not number its cards; thus, listing them is difficult.

PFB

Paul Finkenrath heads a printing company in Berlin, Germany. The firm is best known for its highly embossed and carefully executed cards picturing children, animals, and religious themes. Many of these cards picture a child about an inch tall, next to an animal or object which is disproportionately a couple of inches tall. Fantasy sets, such as the Moon-Faced Men and the exaggerated or disproportional Easter egg cards, are among the most popular.

Raphael Tuck and Sons

In 1866 in a small shop in the Bishopsgate section of London, Raphael Tuck and his wife Ernestine began what was to become the pre-eminent name in English postcard publishing. Originally, the couple turned to

THESE GAY NIMBLE NICKS HAVE COME TO SAY I WISH YOU LOADS OF FUN ON CHRISTMAS DAY

printers in Germany for production of cards and stationery, which Tuck sold both from the shop and from a barrow he himself pushed.

By 1871, their three sons had joined the firm, and that year they published their first Christmas greeting. Son Adolf Tuck launched the first Tuck competition for amateur and professional artists in 1880. Entrants submitted original designs and art that were judged by members of the Royal Academy of Art. Since Raphael Tuck & Sons prided itself on its choice of subject matter and production quality, many of its cards— even artistically rendered view cards—were signed.

WHITNEY-MADE NIMBLE NICKS ARE PLAYING THE HOOP GAME WHICH WAS QUITE POPULAR BETWEEN 1880–1920. ★

A Joyful Easter

Four years later, Adolf, ever the entrepreneur, produced a postcard sold only at the top of Mount Snowden in Wales—a considerable hike just to purchase a postcard!

In 1898, Tuck printed its first numbered series of postcards, a set of twelve lithographed vignette views of London. The Tower of London was the number one card. In 1900, Tuck entered the American postcard market and opened a New York office. American artists illustrated the cards. They were printed in Germany and England, then returned to the U.S. for sale. Tuck continued to flourish in the printing business for many years.

Disastrously, on December 29, 1940, Tuck joined the countless victims of the London Blitz. All the family could salvage from the ruins of the Nazi bombing were the Royal Warrants from Queen Victoria and a handful of other papers. Original paintings, machinery, lithographic stones from which cards were printed, the correspondence, and the day-to-day history of the company were destroyed. What did remain was the legacy of millions of cards

PFB 8294 RELIEF

NEWLY HATCHED CHILDREN ARE PLAYING IN THE NEST. THIS IS NOT AN EVERY DAY SIGHT THESE DAYS AND MAY HAVE NOT BEEN THEN EITHER! ★

sent by mail over the years to collectors' homes in the four corners of the world.

Today, thanks to John Smith and other Tuck collectors, we have a relatively complete checklist of Tuck sets. That after all these years the cards are avidly collected and cherished is a tribute to a company that excelled in producing quality cards from the best original contemporary art.

Tuck postcards are easily identified with their distinctive signature: Art Publishers to Their Majesties the King and Queen.

Tuck, which was taken over by Purnell & Sons, continued producing postcards up to the coronation of the present Queen in 1953.

Williamsburg Art Company

This Brooklyn, New York, firm was a major producer of Jewish New Year and Jewish-related cards. In the 1980s, a major inventory of its cards was discovered. Because of high demand, it is once again difficult to find cards distributed by Williamsburg.

ABOVE: TUCK EASTER FROLIC SERIES 755. THE CONCEPT OF "LIGHT AS A FAIRY" WOULD HAVE TO APPLY HERE FOR THE FLUFFY LITTLE CHICKS TO BE ABLE TO SUPPORT HER WEIGHT. ★

LEFT: PFB 8270.

THIS EGG, THE PERFECT SHAPE, SYMBOL OF LIFE, HAS NOT HAD TIME TO BE DYED AND DECORATED. ★

Introduction to Holidays

The HOLIDAY postcard is unique in the way it reaches out and encompasses the art, traditions, beliefs, mores, and customs of an era. The greeting card was often used as a gift. Certainly, plain inexpensive cards were abundant but beautifully designed ones cost more and could cost up to ten cents—at a time when most people made less than ten dollars a month. The Golden Age of the holiday postcard is the graphically exciting era between 1900 and 1918. There were cards produced before that with great merit and others after that, which were superb, but these were the years when the major publishers were vying for market shares to appease a world that had gone postcard crazy.

Postcards were sent in such abundance that it was like using the telephone today. Mail was delivered three to five times a day, depending on location. A card could be sent in the morning inviting someone to a party that same evening. Not only would the card be delivered that same day, but the reply would be, too. Parties were a major form of recreation and the postcard was a wonderful way to invite someone.

Postcard clubs were formed and people joined pen pal clubs who would then exchange cards with their pen pals, friends, and family. Whole families would sit about and look at the cards they had received, and then spend the rest of their evening sending out replies.

There is still so much interest in postcards that they are being reproduced after a fashion to charm yet another century of recipients and collectors. The colors, styles, and sentiments on these cards is, and remains, timeless.

ELLEN CLAPSADDLE SIGNED CARD OF AN IRISH ST. PATRICK'S DAY OUTING ON A DIRIGIBLE CALLED THE SHAMROCK! ★★

Symbolism and How it is Depicted in Art

I T IS no mystery why postcard artists used symbolism to express their thoughts. The Easter Rabbit represented reproduction and fertility - the abundance of both earth and humankind. The sun was life, the rain refreshment. Even the flowers themselves were given important roles to play in the language of love. If you sent one flower it meant one thing and a different flower meant another - forget-me-nots meant just that and the rose meant something quite different. Symbolism was carried to such extremes that even the

FLORENCE BAMBERGER IS THE PUBLISHER OF THIS ZANY RENDITION OF WITCHES FLYING OFF TO VISIT A JACK-O-LANTERN MOON! ★★★

The·Holly·&·Mistletoe·Waits·

direction you placed your stamp upon a postcard was a message. It was lovely to be told I like you, love you, miss you, care for you, hope you prosper, need you for my friend, and it was said symbolically in cards all the time. It was also nice to have sent a card to declare your feelings. Oh, the relief of wearing one's heart on one's sleeve or telling a friend that you are thankful they are your friend.

WILDT & KRAY 2196.

FANTASY AT ITS VERY BEST AS THIS 1911 CARD ANTHROPOMORPHIZES THE HOLLY AND MISTLETOE INTO MUSICIANS PAR EXCELLENCE. ★★

TUCK'S NO. 531 WAS PART OF THE
CHRISTMAS CHILDREN SERIES.
1. THESE CHILDREN ARE PLAYING UNDER THE
PROTECTIVE HOLLY. ★   2. RARE UNMARKED
WINSCH PUBLISHING CARD. THERE IS
MISCHIEF A-BREW IN THIS LITTLE BOY'S EYES.
WE CAN ONLY GUESS WHAT HE IS UP TOO! AND
THAT GOES FOR HIS LITTLE CAT, TOO! ★★★★★★★

1

2

All Good befortune you,
.. and every day .....
Some ray of golden light
..fall on your way. ... Whittier.

Mistletoe

THE MISTLETOE was the most sacred of all plants to the Druids. The word Druid is a Celtic word meaning "through knowledge, or those whose knowledge is great." It is from the word Druidae, of which the "dru" part was derived from the oak tree that was sacred to them. The acorn was an important source of food to these ancient people and the oak god was the father of all gods. Both words "Celt" and "kilt" come from the same source, which means to hide or conceal. The ancient Celts held the mistletoe in such high esteem that it could only be harvested by the chief Druid at certain times of the year. A golden scythe was used and the mistletoe was never allowed to touch the ground. Though the berries are poisonous,

ELLEN H. CLAPSADDLE NO. 3597

BY INTERNATIONAL ART.

A FASHIONABLE WOMAN ADORNED WITH MISTLETOE.

THE VERSE IS BY THE POET WHITTIER. ★★

A HAPPY NEW YEAR

the plant was known as a cure-all. Science is just beginning to probe the benefits of this parasitic plant that is usually found in oak and apple trees.

In Victorian times, the hanging mistletoe enabled a rather stuffy and moralistic society to relax a few rules and allow public contact between the sexes in an acceptable manner. Mistletoe was placed in a prominent position and games and forfeits were eagerly played and paid under it. It is said that the sweetness of a kiss given under the mistletoe will last the life of the giver.

The misconception that Druids lived only in England and Ireland causes some confusion. The historian Pliny is the only early source to mention mistletoe during Roman times and it is said that the plant was not introduced into Ireland until the 18th century. We can, therefore, assume that there were Druids as far away as Lithuania, Greece, and Egypt. If mistletoe was used, it was brought in or Pliny was speaking of the Druids of Germany who tended sacred groves and ritually cut the mistletoe from the oak trees. Even today, mistletoe is a popular decoration appearing on holiday postcards.

1908 ASTI TYPE BEAUTIFUL WOMAN FRAMED BY HOLLY AND MISTLETOE. ★★

Holly

Holly was considered a holy plant and many churches in England had holly trees and bushes growing on their grounds. With its shiny green leaves and scarlet berries, it was used to decorate the churches at Christmastime. A female holly plant, larger of the two, cannot produce berries without a male plant nearby (know as a bull).

Here is the song of the Holly Fairy which appears in a book by Cecily Mary Barker:

O, I am green in winter-time,
When other trees are brown;
Of all the trees (so saith the rhyme)
The holly bears the crown.
December days are drawing near,

SERIES 1480 PRINTED IN GERMANY.

THE BEAUTIFUL SANTA FACE SURROUNDED BY HOLLY IS REMINISCENT OF THE "GREEN MAN" OR PAGAN GOD OF THE TREES AND FORESTS THAT ONE SEES IN EARLY CHURCH ARCHITECTURE. ★★★

When I shall come to town, and carol-boys
  go singing clear
Of all the trees (o hush and hear!)
For those so well-beloved and merry
As the scarlet Holly Berry?

A postcard rhyme was this:

When Adam met Eve in the Garden,
They thought fig leaves were jolly.

I wonder what they would have thought
If ther'ed been no leaves, but Holly!

During the Saturnalia, the merry festival of Saturn celebrated in December, Romans sent sprigs of holly to their friends. Holly is the masculine of the evergreens, whereas Ivy is the feminine. They are often pictured together, a positioning reflected in the Christmas song, "The Holly and the Ivy."

L&E SERIES 2264, HB GRIGGS

1. JACK HORNER SITS IN FRONT OF HOLLY WALLPAPER. THE JACK HORNER PIES WERE GIVEN AT CHRISTMAS FULL OF PLUMS AND SOMETIMES WITH A SPECIAL SOMETHING LIKE A COIN IN THEM. LATER THERE WERE NOVELTY PIES MADE OF PAPER MACHE. ★ 2. PFB 9019. HOLLY BENEATH THEM, AN UMBRELLA ABOVE, TINY CHILDREN NESTLE IN BETWEEN, SHELTERED FROM THE SNOW. ★

Bring home
Ye Yule log from
Ye Forest great
To the Hollied
Fireside
There to crackle
Midst Merrie
Flames to greet
The Christmas
Tide.

Yule Log

Heap on more wood, the wind is chill;
But let it whistle as it will
We'll keep our Christmas Merry still.

The Yule log was the bringer of warmth and cheer. Only the mightiest and largest oak was used for that purpose.

Where is the Yule log to fill our halls with
*   cheer?*
All the feast is waiting,
Piled high is the board;
Boar's head and peacock
And the garden's hoard,
Soon the guests are coming:
Bards their lays indite;
Where is the Yule log that gives us
*   warmth and light?*

Ah, if the writer of this poem had only known to look on postcards he or she would have known the answer!

NASH PUBLISHING   #C-95 CIRCA 1911.

THE YULE LOG IS OFTEN SHOWN WITH A CHILD RIDING ON IT INDICATING PURITY, LOVE, AND PRO-TECTION. ★

The Egg

Asymbol of life and rejuvenation, the egg was considered by the ancients to be the perfect form. In postcard art, the egg lends itself to fantasy by "eggs-agerating" its size so that it is larger than the hen that laid it. Decorated eggs can be turned into a house for elves or critters to live in; beautiful women can pop out of them just as easily as a chick can. They are even transformed into automobiles for elves!

PFB 5923

BOY SHEPHERD CARRIES A LARGE PINK EGG ON HIS BACK. HIS FLOWERED STAFF IS A NICE TOUCH TO THE ARTISTIC MERIT OF THE CARD AND IS A SYMBOL OF SPRING. ★

A Happy New Year

We celebrate New Year's Eve on December 31 and New Year's Day on January 1. New Year's cards were intended for the day when most inclusive family celebrations occurred. Some ethnic groups are fortunate to have their own special day so they celebrate twice. Chinese New Year and Jewish New Year are two such holidays that separate postcards have been produced for. Those that are interested further will have to go looking for them at a Deltiological Bourse, or postcard show.

Unfortunately, many of the smaller or ethnic holidays have been omitted as there simply isn't space for them in this volume.

New Year's Eve and Day

SERIES 629

ARTIST ALF SCHONIAN. DWARF RIDING A PIG AMIDST THE MAGIC MUSHROOMS AND TOSSING LUCKY SYMBOLS INTO THE AIR. ★★★

NEW YEAR'S RESOLUTION

RESOLVED
TO GET
THE BEST
OF EVERY
ARGUMENT
THIS YEAR

WHITNEY CARD

SNOW PEOPLE OFF FOR A STROLL. ★★

The symbols for the New Year are Father Time, hoary with age, being replaced by the newborn child. It is the retelling of the King who dies only to be replaced with a younger and stronger ruler. It is the story of the Phoenix shedding his beautiful feathers and then bursting into flames only to be reborn from the ashes of his self-induced pyre. It is senility and decay replaced by virility. Prosperity and renewal are the wishes of the day—to be perpetuated throughout the year.

The symbols of prosperity are many and we will see them repeated again and again during the year on other holiday cards. The four-leaf clover, pigs, mushrooms, black cats, chimney sweeps, stars, and goats are but a few of these symbols that induce and indicate prosperity and happiness.

Seasonal figures such as snowmen cavort and frolic with elves and animals as well as children and adults. Snow people tend to have real character and most are lifelike rather than immobile ice figures. Because of the Nordic influence on American culture we often find elves, gnomes, trolls, and goats included with the traditional seasonal figures. Elves and gnomes usually dominate postcards produced for Scandinavian countries. These mystical people vary in size and character depending on what they are called and where they come from. Gnomes, elves, and dwarfs are very different in build and facial features, and ethnically vary.

Don't confuse a dwarf from the Black Forests of Germany with the tiny elfin sprites of the British Isles or the petite, knobby-kneed Scandinavian elves with the wrinkled, elderly faces or innocent child like ones that Artist Jenny Nyström and other Nordic artists made so famous. These elves with their red hats are called Tomtens and became a favorite of the Pennsylvania Dutch. The usage of these beings, along with the pig and four-leaf clover, give an almost international flavor to the holiday. It might be useful to know that though most of these cards were done by Swedish artists

in Sweden. During this time Sweden was the predominant power in the region and their influence was felt not only politically and economically, but culturally as well all over Scandinavia and well beyond.

Year date cards were extremely popular for a while and certain years such as 1908, 1909, 1910, 1911, and 1912 were quite popular. These can be mundane numbers or they can be fancifully executed people or animals in such positions that they actually become the numbers.

The New Year is supposed to be a sweeping away of the pains and trials of the previous year thus allowing people a chance to begin with a clean slate. Even with all the good wishes that are sent via these cards, there is little chance to begin fresh but with a resolution or two and a bit of determination that the new year can be better than the old. The Chinese celebrate their holiday with dragons, which bring good luck, and with firework displays and parades. The Jewish New Year is considerably more religious than the secular holiday that is celebrated by most groups. There are precious few cards for Chinese New Year but many were made for the Jewish New Year including some done by the famous Wiener Werkstatte. This was the Vienna workshops, which in the last quarter of the 19th century used the motto "To age it is art, to art it is freedom." The Secessionists and

TUCK PUBLISHING, CIRCA 1911, SET NO. 605

THE SANDS OF TIME TRICKLE THROUGH THE HOURGLASS, UNENDING MOVEMENT AND A REMINDER THAT NO ONE CAN STOP TIME. ★★

PENNIES MAY FALL FROM HEAVEN WHEN IT RAINS BUT THE NEW YEAR'S ELF
POURS GOLD AND SILVER COINS AND THE GOOD LUCK HORSESHOES UPON THOSE
THEY WISH SEASON GREETINGS UPON. THE KEEPER OF THE KEYS OF
PROSPERITY IS SITTING ON HALEYS COMET WHICH DATES THE CARD TO 1910. ★★

artists like Mela Kola, Gustav Klimt, Oskar Kokoschka Egon Schiele, and Koloman Moser were at the heart of this movement.

Regardless of what country or language the postcard originated from, the greetings and wishes for good luck and happiness predominate. The sentiments of love are an underlying current as celebrators kiss when the transition takes place, under a clock, ever the symbol of fleeting time or under the mistletoe, which is the symbol of everlasting love. Incidentally, the New Year's baby is a clone of Eros or Cupid, the God of love.

One more important connection that must not be forgotten is the Scottish influence. The poet Robert Burns is probably the most quoted poet of all time but he was also the reason much of the early folk music of Scotland survived. He traveled the countryside collecting old tunes and preserving this heritage for posterity. How could any celebration be complete without the singing of his poem "Auld Lang Syne"? The Burns's connection is one of the reasons we see thistle and tartan on New Year's cards. His immortal words are a reminder to remember times that have passed and friends who have departed. It is also a reminder to cherish the friends and loved ones that are still with us. "We'll share a cup of kindness yet in the days of Auld Lang Syne."

DELL'ANNA & GASPARINI CIRCA 1923
NO. 558-3. SIGNED BY BUSI.

1. A NEW YEAR FULL OF LOVE AND ROMANCE ★

2. IT'S MIDNIGHT, THE NEW YEAR ARRIVES AND SO
DOES ONE'S TRUE LOVE WHO WILL BRAVE ALL TO TOAST
THE NEW YEAR IN AND TASTE HIS ADORED ONES KISS.
THE ROMANCE OF THE LADDER AT THE WINDOW HAS
SADLY GONE THE WAY OF MANY A QUAINT AND LOVELY
OLD CUSTOM. ★★

1. NO. 971. CHILD ANGEL LABORS UNDER THE BOUNTY OF A
BASKET OF ROSES. ROSES ARE REMEMBRANCE AND IN SNOW CLAD
DAYS ARE A SIGN OF AFFLUENCE. ★ 2. TUCK SERIES NO. 605. A
PICTURE OF A BEAUTIFUL CHILD WITH A SUNDIAL, WHICH IS THE
SYMBOL OF PASSING TIME. ★ 3. TUCK NO. 501. A CHILD WITH
HIS PUPPY. ANIMALS WERE A VERY POPULAR MOTIF ON POSTCARDS,
ESPECIALLY FOR EVERYDAY POSTINGS. ★

1. E.W. SAVORY, LD OF BRISTOL U.K. PRODUCED THIS "CLIFTON" HAND-COLORED POSTCARD, WHICH WAS ADVERTISED AS "ALL BRITISH FROM START TO FINISH." 2. SERIES NO. 567 IS TYPICAL OF THE HIGH QUALITY ART DECO ART CARD. ARTIST L.E. ★★★★★ EACH

1

1. TUCK #133. FOUR-LEAF CLOVERS AND THE
FERMENTED FRUIT OF THE VINE ARE ENJOYED
AND USED TO MAKE A TOAST BY NAKED YOUTH,
SYMBOLS OF THE NEW YEAR. ★   2. TUCK SERIES N
301 USES FOUR-LEAF CLOVERS AND PIGS TO
ENHANCE THE GOLD YEAR DATE. ★★

2

A Happy
New Year

A HAPPY NEW YEAR

1. CHERUBS ARE PERMITTED TO PRODUCE GOLD
COINS AND ARE GRANTED IMMUNITY UNDER THE
LAW! THESE GOLD COINS ARE NOT FORGERIES BUT
GENUINE NEW YEAR WISHES. ★★   2. SERIES 580
BY JULIEN BIEN PUBLISHING. ONE DOES NOT HAVE
TO GO FAR TO OBTAIN A NEW YEAR KISS AS THIS
MISTLETOE MISS IS READY AND WAITING. ★★

1. A LOVELY EXAMPLE OF AIRBRUSHING WAS DONE ON THIS HEAVILY EMBOSSED YEAR DATE CARD FOR 1908. THE WOMAN IN THE ART NOUVEAU STYLE DANGLES PUPPETS AS THE DATE, WHICH IS IN A FANCIFUL MANNER DEPICTED BY POSITIONED FIGURES. THE COLORS ARE VERY TASTEFUL AND SUBTLE FOR AIRBRUSH WHICH OFTEN TENDS TOWARD THE GARISH. ★★   2. GERMAN PRINTED SERIES 15909. PIGS DRAW A COACH BEARING HOLLY, THE SYMBOL OF PROSPERITY, RACING INTO THE NEW YEAR. ★★   3. GEL GOLD NO. 15910, PRINTED IN GERMANY. ★★

1. HOLD-TO-LIGHT-CARD FOR THE YEAR 1908
WHICH AGAIN SHOWS THE FANCIFUL USE OF
PEOPLE TO PRODUCE THE YEAR NUMBERS. ★★★★
2. CHILDREN IN ETHNIC COSTUMES WERE VERY
POPULAR MOTIFS IN CERTAIN HIGH-ETHNIC
OCCUPANCY AREAS OF THE COUNTRY. HERE THEY
USE A CANNON TO BLOW GREETINGS AND GIFT
WISHES TO THE RECIPIENT. ★   3. THE CORNUCOPIA,
SYMBOL OF PLENTY, IS HELD BY TWO CHERUBS AND
SPRINKLES FORGET-ME-NOTS AND PINK WILD ROSES
UPON THE LAND BELOW. ★

Die besten Glückwünsche zum Neuen Jahre!

Happy New Year

1. SERIES 629. ARTIST ALF SCHONIAN. DWARF
PUSHING A WHEELBARROW WITH SYMBOLS OF
LUCK, PROSPERITY, AND VIRILITY IN IT. ★★★
2. PRINTED IN SAXONY NO. 0640. GELATIN OF
PIGS, GOLD COINS, FORGET-ME-NOTS, AND FOUR-
LEAF CLOVERS WISH, IN SYMBOLS, THE HOPES OF
THE SENDER. ★

1. SERIES 175. IN 1903, WHEN THIS CARD WAS
SENT, AVIATION WAS IN ITS INFANCY AND HAD
CAUGHT THE ROMANTIC FANCY OF THE PUBLIC. A
FLYING MACHINE ADORNED IN FORGET-ME-NOTS
AND FOUR-LEAF CLOVERS AND MANNED BY
TWO PRETTY CHILDREN NOT ONLY HERALDED A
PROSPEROUS NEW YEAR BUT THE ADVANCE OF
TECHNOLOGY. ★   2. EAS PUBLISHING. CHERUB
RING MASTER HAS THE PIGS OF PROSPERITY
JUMPING THROUGH A HOOP AND CARRYING
BAGS OF MONEY. ★★

Valentine's Day

RED AND white are the main colors for Valentine's Day which is filled with passion, lace, and flowers. Pagan deities, Cupid or Eros, rule the day that is dedicated to a Christian martyr, Saint Valentine. He purportedly sent the first valentine during those hair-raising days when chariot contests just weren't enough and lion food was a bit too expensive for the Roman Emperor's budget. Whether the story is true or not, it is consistent with the passion and sentiment of this holiday.

The earliest Valentines were delivered by hand and were often accompanied by a small gift such as flowers or a lace handkerchief. With the arrival of a regulated postal system there was a rapid escalation in the production and sending of valentines.

Though most of the postcards are post-1900, the various types of valentines were in great demand long before then. Lacy valentines, beautifully lithographed cards, ones that opened up with honeycomb hearts, or with die-cut cupids and children, are all part of the evolution of the holiday (even those that were intended to insult). The styles and types varied from country to country and even from region to region. One story claims that an Australian miner had an exceedingly large valentine of solid gold made! This probably would have been just post-1900, when large mining fortunes were being made. Cobweb valentines, which had a string attached to the center, would be pulled gently forwards to reveal a picture underneath. Sailor-made valentines from seashells and seaweed—sometimes even carved into whalebone or ivory—are very desirable. In Germany, Austria, and the United Kingdom, lovely die-cut and lithographed valentines were produced. Here in America, Esther Howland began hand-cutting lace valentines that were later machine produced by the Whitney Company.

The evolution of the valentine has been one of devolution as the quality has progressively gone from being inventive,

PFB SERIES 6859 CIRCA 1910. THE MAN IN THE MOON PROVIDED A GRAND PLACE TO SPOON (KISS). MOON FACES ARE A COLLECTING CATEGORY BY THEMSELVES. ★★

esthetic works of art that were cherished and kept for generations, to mass-produced printed matter of sometimes dubious artistic merit. Flowers, hearts, cherubs, and/or cupids predominate and act as a foil for beautiful women and lovely girls. On the other hand, there are old maids, fat men, love-starved maidens and matrons, and gormless men with little means and even less hair. Valentines go from the highly ornate and romantic to insult and derision of types of people and professions.

THE PENNY DREADFUL, or Vinegar Valentine, was sent to people whose feelings one wanted to hurt. They were very popular at one time. Not only were they sent to flirts, social climbers, cads, gamblers, braggarts, and thieves, but also they targeted professionals such as doctors, lawyers, judges, butchers, politicians, teachers, suffragettes, policemen, and golfers. These were sent anonymously and it was a grand way to let some lawyer know you thought him a sleaze or a judge dishonest. Unfortunately, many a spinster schoolteacher received them from students because she was an easy target for schoolboy pranks. Just as the suffragette was branded as a menace to society because of

PFB NO. MAN AND WOMAN SIT ON THE MOON

WHILE OLD MAN MOON SMILES AT THEM LIGHTING

UP THE NIGHT. SERIES 6859. CIRCA 1910★★

THE BROKER

You call yourself a broker,
You two-for-fiver smoker.
Instead of widow-choker;
You always take what'er we make,

Jeune homme à moitié piqué, mais intelligent et chic, aimant le pinard, désire union avec demoiselle distinguée, tenant commerce de spiritueux, où il pourrait rendre service à la dégustation.

Ecrire à Zizi Duchenoque,
Villa la Cuite, La Vasée-sur-Mer.

117

1. AUROCROME SERIES, PENNY DREADFULS, OR VINEGAR VALENTINES, WERE OFTEN SENT TO PEOPLE ONE DIDN'T LIKE OR TO SHOW A DISDAIN OF THEIR PROFESSION AND THE WAY THEY PRACTICED IT. ★   2. NUMBER 117. REGARDLESS OF WHAT LANGUAGE IT WAS WRITTEN IN OR IN WHAT COUNTRY IT WAS SENT, THE PENNY DREADFUL WAS AN INSULT INTENDED AND AN INSULT TAKEN. ★

the prejudice against her gender, the eccentric and those who lived outside of society's rules were vilified more than crooked public servants and cheating merchants. An unmarried woman and a suffragette were both a disgrace to society and more vilified than lawbreakers. Reading the insults and barbed comments are fun now but were hardly a pleasant thing to have slipped under your door or delivered by the mailman. The earliest versions of these were not in postcard form and were sent out to the recipients. Later, Congress passed a law that the sender, rather than the recipient, should have to pay the postage. Can you imagine having to pay the mailman for your mail only to find it was someone insulting you? It would be like paying to get junk mail or a dunning letter from a solicitor.

Because the Penny Dreadful is not as graphically beautiful as the cards we have shown here, it seems almost a necessity to quote a few of them for your amusement:

An actor, who thought he could act,
Did his best applause to attract:
"My art's ripe!" he cried.
But the people replied "It's rotten!"
And it was for a fact.

Or

Spencer Spender not a cent
Does he put by to pay the rent:

Unless he'll to our pleadings yield
He'll surely end in Potters field!
Are you a Spencer Spender?

Or

Stop looking in windows and gadding
*   around;*
Your neck's made of rubber, your brain is
*   not sound.*
You never buy dry goods or anything nice
You only go looking and haven't the price!

And these are some of the "nicer" ones so you can imagine how awful some of the others were! Penny Dreadfuls were seldom kept if received. They were too embarrassing if anyone saw that you had received one. It is surprising to find that one was postally used and kept.

Valentines ran the entire gambit from ornate to simple, from handmade to mass produced, from poetic to baby talk, from nice to nasty, and from loving to begging to be loved. The sentiment on the cards was sometimes long and embellished, sometimes short and cute. One example of a nice one:

To My Valentine. I love you more than
peach ice cream. I love you more than
candy. I think you're just a Cracker-Jack.
I think your fine and dandy.

1. VENUS AMIDST THE FLOWERS WITH HER BASKET OF HEARTS IS
THE MOTHER OF CUPID AND THE GODDESS OF LOVE. IT IS SURPRISING
THAT SHE IS SO SELDOM SEEN EXCEPT IN HER MORE WORLDLY
FORM. ★★   2. SERIES 675. EMBOSSED AND GOLD ENHANCED CUPID. ★
3. WINSCH PUBLISHING 1912. THE WOMAN IN THE HEART IS BY ARTIST
SAMUEL SCHMUCKER AND THE BALANCE OF THE CARD MAY HAVE BEEN
DONE BY SOMEONE ELSE THAT JOHN WINSCH EMPLOYED. ★★

WINSCH MECHANICAL 1912.

WHEN TAB IS PULLED UP BEHIND THE HEART A
LITTLE GIRL APPEARS AND THEY KISS. ★★★

My Valentine Wish

May Life ever bring You
but Sunshine and Laughter;
Hope follow You still
and no Sorrow ❧ ❧ ❧
come after.

St. Valentine Greets You

'Tis pleasant to
think of Hearts
kind and true,
And that is
the Reason I'm
thinking of you.

TUCK SERIES 221

THE MELANCHOLY MUSIC OF LOVE, THE FRAGILITY

AND DELICACY OF A BUTTERFLY, AND THE AROMA

OF FLOWERS; THE HEARTS AND FLOWERS OF THIS

DAY ARE SACRED TO SAINT VALENTINE. ★★ EACH

My Heart is thine sweet Valentine.

Love's Greeting

To My Valentine

LA ROSE

1. GERMAN PRINTED CARD WHICH IS
PROBABLY BY ARTIST ELLEN CLAPSADDLE. ★
2. INTERNATIONAL ART CARD THAT IS HEAVILY
ENHANCED WITH SILVER. THE ELEGANCE OF AN
EARLIER ERA WAS CONSIDERED VERY ROMANTIC
IN EDWARDIAN TIMES. ★★   3. NOVELTY ART
NOUVEAU CARD WITH INSERT MIRROR HEART
NO. 230 KUNSTVERLAG J.W. HAEG 1900 BONN,
GERMANY. ★★★★

I'm trying so hard to forget you.

1. THIS TAGGART PUBLISHING CARD CIRCA 1909
IS PURE FANTASY IN DESIGN BUT PERHAPS NOT
IN THE MESSAGE THAT IS BEING SENT. ★
2. THE FORTUNE VALENTINE SERIES SHOWS
THE QUEEN OF HEARTS AND WHAT A GAMBLE
LOVE IS. ★★

1. SPOONER & BARTON, SERIES 696. CUPID AS
A BLACKSMITH WORKS VERY HARD FORGING
RINGS OF LOVE THAT ARE UNBREAKABLE. THIS
REPRESENTS THE DIVINE STRENGTH OF LOVE. ★

2. SERIES 208. A HORSELESS CARRIAGE DRIVEN BY
A BEAUTY AND DIRECTED BY A CARNATION-HATTED
CUPID DANGLING A HEART. ★★

1. INTERNATIONAL ART CHILDREN ELOPING.

PROBABLY BY ARTIST ELLEN CLAPSADDLE. ★

2. SERIES 7904 PRINTED IN GERMANY HAS A SILK

APPLIED OUTFIT ON THE CUPID POSTPERSON.

THESE SILK CARDS COMMANDED A PREMIUM WHEN

THEY WERE NEW. ★★

To my Valentine

THE flag beneath whose spreading folds
True hearts are bound together;
May yours and mine Sweet Valentine,
Be bound to-day for ever.

K ♥

1554   COPYRIGHTED 1905 BY ULLMAN MFG.CO.,N.Y.
KING OF HEARTS

❷

1. PATRIOTISM AND THE LOVE CUPID BRINGS ARE

INTERTWINED ON ST. VALENTINE'S DAY. ★★

2.ULLMAN PUBLISHING 1905 SERIES 1554. CUPID IS

THE KING OF HEARTS AND HIS BOW AND ARROW ARE

AIMED DIRECTLY AT THE RECIPIENT'S HEART. ★★★

1. GIBSON SERIES 415. A SWEET YOUNG DUTCH
BOY TO STEAL YOUR HEART AWAY. ★   2. TUCK
SERIES 104 WOODEN WOOERS. DUTCH CHILDREN
WERE QUAINT AND OFTEN DEPICTED ON CARDS AS
THEY APPEALED TO THE PENNSYLVANIA DUTCH
WHO ARE REALLY GERMAN. ★★

Nothing slow for the like of us.

Saint Patrick's Day

MANY PEOPLE are very surprised that this day, when all of America waxes green, the cards were produced almost exclusively for the United States. Even today the many postcard collectors in Ireland turn up their noses at these cards and consider them "foreign." They are one of the most undervalued categories on the market today, which is surprising considering how well executed the graphics are and how many Irish there are in this country.

The cards that are most eagerly sought after are by important artists such as Samuel Schmucker, Ellen Clapsaddle, Gene Carr, Freixsas, and A. Heinmuller. Schmucker's beautiful women are often printed on silk and used as inserts. His Saint Patrick's Day cards are some of the few where you will find a small "SLS" signature. Gene Carr, on the other hand, made his Irish folks look as simian as possible, poking Darwinian fun at their evolution. It is amazing that they were so popular with the Irish themselves when they came onto the market. Perhaps, the fact one can laugh at oneself or how others see you is the basis for this, or possibly the fact that many Irish descendants thought this was what leprechauns looked like. It was, and may still be, a mortal sin to have traffic with the wee people, and these might be human-sized leprechauns, which seems a mite deceptive. There is much controversy about Carr's work.

Considering the fact that most of these were sent from one Irish-American to another, it is surprising to see that stereotypes do abound: the Irish Colleen, beautiful as the gold of Tara; the drunken Irishman as a wastrel, loafer, and scoundrel; and the hard-working, elderly pipe-smoking old lady that carried home sticks on her back or peat from the bog to keep the cottage warm.

SERIES #1450

INTERNATIONAL ART PUBLISHING SIGNED BY ARTIST ELLEN CLAPSADDLE TWO BEAUTIFUL IRISH CHILDREN STAND IN FRONT OF THE FLAG OF IRELAND. ★★

Let Erin Remember

Ellen M Clapsaddle

What color should be seen,
Where our father's homes have been,
But our own immortal Green.

Donkey carts, spinning wheels, and the poems of Eva Brennen were meant to make the reader nostalgic for the old country and old ways of life. But if this was idealizing the land of their ancestors, it certainly was no incentive to go back and live there. The cards were inserted vignettes of scenic splendor and were often made of printed silk, usually with a decorative border of shamrocks or little gold pigs.

The pig was just as important a symbol on Saint Patrick's Day cards as were shamrocks. If you owned a pig, you were fairly prosperous and would not go hungry. A sow with many piglets was real wealth. Ask a farmer in any agrarian society how important the owning of animals are, whether they be pigs, chickens, or cows. "Pigs root ahead, while fowl scratch behind" is an old folk saying. The pig is also quite adept in finding mushrooms and truffles, which are lucky symbols and valuable commodities, as well as tasting delicious. The shamrock meant luck but the pig meant life itself.

Every now and then, one sees a card with an add-on metal pig or a small bag of shamrock seeds, purportedly from Ireland, attached to it. Novelty cards were very popular and this is the only category you will find cards made out of peat. These cards are

INTERNATIONAL ART NO. 931 A PRETTY WOMAN

WEARING THE GREEN BY ELLEN CLAPSADDLE. ★

usually a dark brownish or dark green color. Many postcard dealers file them in their novelty section. The idea of these cards were so that the recipient could have a small piece of his home of ancestry to keep near his heart so he would not get homesick.

The figure of Saint Patrick himself is seldom seen on cards extolling his day. When he does show up he looks either like Father Christmas (not the jolly fat man but the saint) or like a Druid of old with white flowing robes, a white flowing beard, and a bishops miter on his head. Some histories actually have him as a Druid that converted to Christianity.

There is a lot of Pagan influence in the depiction of Saint Patrick. Interestingly enough, in J.R.R. Tolkien's *The Hobbit* and his trilogy, *The Lord of the Rings*, Gandalf or Mithrander appear much the same. The scarcest of these depictions appear as hold-to-light cards, a category many collect for their novelty and beauty, regardless of subject.

In the early 1900s the evolution of this

SPOONER & BARTON SERIES 7041 IS
ONE OF THE FEW CARDS OF SAINT
PATRICK HIMSELF.

IT SEEMS STRANGE THAT HE SHOULD SHOW UP SO
SELDOM ON CARDS FOR HIS OWN DAY. HE LOOKS
VERY MUCH LIKE SANTA CLAUS. ★★

THE HARP THAT PLAYED IN TARA'S HALLS AND
SHAMROCKS BRING LUCK AS WELL AS GREETINGS.

★★

holiday was woven together with the growth of the labor movement, the plight of the miners, and the growth of the Molly Maguires organization. The controversy over the Maguires still rages on. Were they the champions of the abused miners who were framed and hung? Were the murderers and assassins the railroad, the mine owners, and the Pinkertons? One thing is for certain; they were nothing like their depiction in the Sean Connery movie *The Molly Maguires*. Perhaps no one will know the true story as the official records are mysteriously missing. Let it suffice saying that the holiday assumed a political and social significance because of this and that it has little to do with the color green, snakes, or saints. Rather, it can be seen in the gathering of the laborers and workers of all faiths and nationalities and their participation in the parades every March 17th.

One last symbol that should be acknowledged is the depiction of pipes and harps on many of these cards. The harp is the legendary one that was played in ancient Ireland before the King when he sat in Tara's hall. This tradition dates back to the Stone Age in Ireland and included a long line of different Kings. With the renewed interest in Celtic music since the late 1950s, the tradition of harping has taken on a very significant role once again. The Bards, an order of Druids, were the last

of that ancient order to be persecuted by the incoming Romans and Christians. The legendary halls of Tara still ring with their music in the hearts and minds of the poetically inclined. The pipe, on the other hand, was clay. Tobacco is relatively modern, as it did not reach the British Isles until Sir Walter Raleigh brought it for Queen Elizabeth I upon his return from America. Pipes were smoked by both men and women. Sometimes they dominate an entire card by themselves. Sometimes it is referred to as an Irish Peace Pipe and on one card there is an American Indian and an Irishman together with their respective peace pipes. This was not only the inexpensive comfort of the poor, but it meant they also had sufficient food and prosperity to be able to afford a wee bit of luxury.

The dominant color of this holiday is green as it heralds the coming spring that will turn the barren winter ravaged land back to green.

1. WINSCH PUBLISHING 1914 450/45 NO. 65827
THE LADY OF THE SHAMROCKS GROWING OUT OF
A WOODEN FLOWER BARREL WITH A LITTLE BOY.
ERIN GO BRAGH = IRELAND'S MY HOMELAND.
FOUR LEAF-CLOVERS FOR EXTRA LUCK AT TOP AND
BOTTOM OF CARD. ★★★   2. WINSCH 1914 450/45
NO. 65827. LITTLE BOY LOOKING LIKE A
LEPRECHAUN FIDDLES WHILE LITTLE RED-HEADED
COLLEEN DANCES A JIG. FOUR-LEAF CLOVERS ARE
PRESENT FOR GOOD LUCK. ★★★

1. WINSCH PUBLISHING 1914. THESE JASON FREIXSAS CHILDREN ARE DANCING FOR JOY BECAUSE OF ALL OF THE LUCKY SHAMROCKS THEY HAVE GROWING IN THEIR POT. ★★★

2. ELLEN CLAPSADDLE, INTERNATIONAL ART. ★

1. BARTON AND SPOONER S 413 B SAINT PATRICK'S
DAY PARADES WOULDN'T BE AS GOOD WITHOUT A
DRUMMER LIKE THIS ONE WHICH IS PROBABLY BY
ARTIST BERNHARDT WALL. ★   2. BARTON AND
SPOONER S 413B PRINTED IN USA. THE ARTIST IS
PROBABLY BERNHARDT WALL. ★

1. THIS 1914 CARD, SERIES #4 SHOWS UNCLE SAM
WITH HIS GOOD FRIEND AND DRINKING PARTNER
TOASTING IN THIS MOST IMPORTANT DAY. MANY
IRISH AMERICANS WISHED AMERICA WOULD MAKE
IRELAND A STATE! ★★   2. SERIES #4 SHAMROCKS
AND A CLAY PIPE SMOKER GREET ONE IN FRONT
OF A LUCKY HORSESHOE. ★

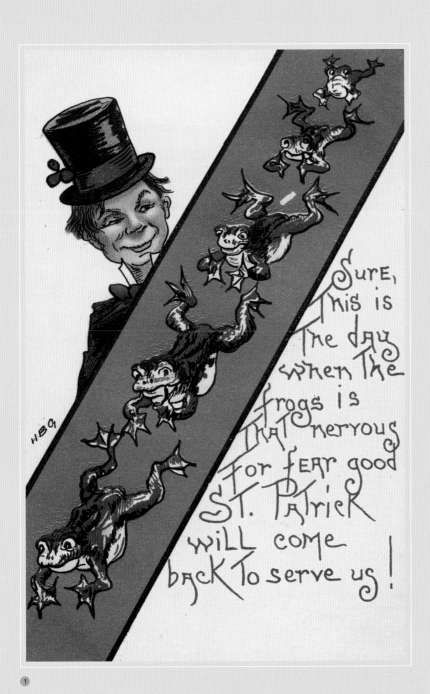

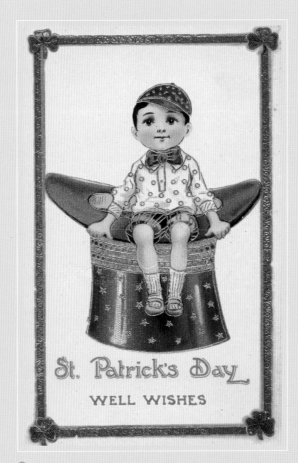

1. HB GRIGG'S STYLE IS UNMISTAKABLE WITH THE MANY LETTERS AND WHIMSICAL RENDITIONS. FROGS ARE GREEN, THE WHOLE WORLD IS GREEN ON ST. PADDY'S DAY. ★★   2. A BARTON AND SPOONER CARD OF A LITTLE BOY, MOST LIKELY BY ARTIST BERNHARDT WALL. GELATIN FINISH WITH GOLD ENHANCEMENT. ★

As our flag floats out on the breeze
Memories fly back to me keen
For again I'm a lass, gathering shamrocks
In a frock all made in green.

1. UNSIGNED WINSCH BY ARTIST SAMUEL SCHMUCKER.

BEAUTIFUL COLLEEN SITS ON A SHAMROCK CHAIR

WITH HER FEET FIRMLY PLANTED ON IRELAND. ★★★

2. A NICELY EMBOSSED AND SILVER ENHANCED CARD

OF A BEAUTIFUL COLLEEN CARRYING AN IRISH FLAG. ★

1. UNSIGNED WINSCH BY ARTIST SAMUEL SCHMUCKER. A BEAUTIFUL COLLEEN HUGGING A LUCKY PIG, WHICH IS HALF GOLDEN, AND WEARING A GREEN BOW, TO GIVE THE IMPRESSION THAT THIS IS IRELAND'S LUCKY PIG. A SHAMROCK WREATH WITH A SHOWER OF GOLD IS BEHIND HER AND THE GOLDEN HARP THAT IN TARA'S HALLS WAS PLAYED BY THE DRUIDIC BARDS OF LONG AGO IS ON HER FROCK. ★★★   2. CIRCA 1910 UNSIGNED WINSCH BY ARTIST SAMUEL SCHMUCKER. SHAMROCKS, CLAY PIPES, GREEN (THE EMERALD ISLE'S COLOR), AND AN IRISH COLLEEN ARE TO MANY WHAT THIS DAY IS ALL ABOUT. ★★★

All Easter Joys be Thine

Easter

(A moveable date depending on which calendar is used. On the first Sunday after the full moon, on the next Sunday after March 21, or one week later if the full moon falls on a Sunday.)

GOTTSCHAULK AND DREFFUS 2161. ★

THOUGH THERE are many religious cards for Easter, they are few in contrast to those with a secular theme. It seems as though the religious aspect is relegated to mourning and fasting on Good Friday and Easter is supposed to be the harbinger of spring—a time to feast and parade around in new clothing. The date of Easter was moved to coincide with that of the celebration of the Goddess Oester and the return of life to the barren lands that had tasted the snow and cold of the winter months. That which died was reborn and, hence, the egg became the symbol of everlasting life and a frequently found item on Easter cards.

Before Easter egg dye came on the market, onion peel was saved and then boiled, and the eggs were put in the water, soon to become a rich maroon. Members of the Armenian Apostolic and Greek Orthodox churches still carry on this tradition.

It is interesting to note that before Peter Cottontail and the Easter Bunny, eggs were gathered by hens, children, and dwarves; often those they had decorated and were gathering were overwhelmingly out of proportion with the gatherer. This adds a charming, fantasy quality to the art which at times borders on the surrealistic. Add to this animals dressed in the height of human fashion and the fantasy of the holiday seems to overshadow everything else. Cherry and apple trees blossom and occasionally the face of a beautiful nymph can be seen amidst the flowers. Lilies and other individual spring flowers reveal the faces of lovely women or children that sway with the breeze on their delicate stalks. Little girls and young maidens dance with dwarves and bunnies while little boys use sheep-drawn carts to transport a single colored egg (whose size in proportion to the child and sheep would have been half a ton). The fantasy works because it is so well designed and is esthetically pleasing. Add gold and silver to these highly embossed cards and they take on a mystical quality.

Perhaps the fabulous Easter eggs were

inspired by the eggs that were made by Faberge for the Russian Royal Family, inset with precious gems, enameled, and made of gold and silver. Even eggs decorated for the common people of Russia and the Ukraine were made of sugar and colored foils that sparkled and glittered.

Schonian and Schlidt, both German artists, drew fanciful decorated eggs, sometimes using Dresden die cuts for embellishment, although examples are somewhat rare.

But the egg is not the alpha and omega of recurring Easter images.

Angels are usually beautiful women or lovely little girls while cherubs are usually

GERMAN AMERICAN NOVELTY ART CARD FROM TSN SERIES 555 SIGNED BY ARTIST ALF SCHONIAN.

THE DWARVES, LOOKING LIKE THEY DWELL IN THE BLACK FOREST, ARE SURROUNDED BY SYMBOLS OF VIRILITY, IMMORTALITY, REBIRTH, AND AWAKENING. THE DWARVES THEMSELVES ARE ONES YOU CAN BELIEVE IN BECAUSE OF THEIR NATURALNESS AND REALISTIC DETAIL. ★★★

A Jouyous Easter

genderless little boys. Angels are usually giving things like baskets of food, toys, eggs, or Christmas trees and speak words of comfort and peace while cherubs go bouncing about like overweight Kewpies without clothing. They don't do much of anything except act as decorations, giving—or getting—kisses. Supposedly there is only one Cupid, except on postcards.

Nature is important in Easter art. The rabbit is a symbol of fertility; therefore, it is usually he who is delivering the eggs. Frequently, cards incorporate flowers such as the lily, snowdrop, and crocus; bushes, like the lilac and forsythia; and flowering trees, such as the apple and cherry. Re-member that this is relating to the art of the postcard and not in reference to cards that show religious versions such as those done by Stengel or others that produced art cards from famous religious paintings and frescos.

Some of the most artistic cards have intricate Art Nouveau designs and flourishes with short but poignant thoughts or wishes, quotes from the Bible, or other lofty sayings. Nister was a master of this style but his cards, though scarce, are not as popular as those with angels or animals.

Just like an Easter egg hunt, you can

NO MATTER HOW SMALL THIS LITTLE GIRL IS, THE HEN THAT LAID THIS EGG WAS WORTH HER WEIGHT IN GOLD. ★

look in impossible places and find something hidden such as dual meanings, Pagan and Christian derivatives, as well as artists letting their fancy run wild.

Scandinavian witches add humor to the holiday and are an anomaly. No home there should be without an Easter Witch that brings good luck and happiness. These witches come in all sizes and ages and have a great fondness for coffee, which they like to brew on rooftops. After they have enjoyed a cup or two, they fly off to the mountain Blakulla where they dance, sing,

and make pots of soup or stew. They are apparently the ancestors of the kitchen witch that migrated from Europe and to the rest of Scandinavia and then on to America. They became popular a few decades ago and continue to protect many a kitchen against burning roasts and boiling-over pots. These cards appear in many sizes not seen for other holidays. Cards by Jenny Nyström are in high demand as are other well-known Scandinavian artists. The idea of witches at Easter is novel, but then much of the Scandinavian art is unique.

ALL JOY TO YOU THIS EASTERTIDE.

Easter Greetings

1. MANY A MAN WOULD ENJOY FINDING SUCH A MAID PEEKING OUT OF HIS EASTER EGG. ★★

2. CIRCA 1907. DRESSED TO THE "NTHS" THIS RABBIT IS TAKING HIS CHICK FOR A WALK. ★★

EASTER GREETING.

A HAPPY EASTER

1. ON A LOVELY SPRING DAY TWO FRIENDS DANCE AWAY
THE HOURS AMID THE FLOWERS. ONE HUMAN, ONE NOT, BUT
BOTH IN THE SPRINGTIME OF THEIR LIVES. ★★   2. BENEATH
THE FLOWERING APPLE TREES THE LONG BEARDED RABBIT
LISTENS TO A LITTLE GIRL TELL HER SECRETS. ★

1. A. WINSCH PUBLISHING EASTER TABLEAU OF A
CURLY-TOPPED CHILD OVERWHELMED BY THE CONCEPT
OF SO MANY CHICKS AND BUNNIES. 1911. ★★
2. BARTON AND SPOONER SERIES 0709 WITH GELATIN
FINISH. IT IS A DIFFICULT JOB DELIVERING EASTER
EGGS, AND IF FATHER RABBIT NEEDS A BIT OF SPIRIT
TO FORTIFY HIMSELF IT IS QUITE UNDERSTANDABLE.
IN THE REALM OF FANTASY MOST THINGS CAN BE
JUSTIFIED. ★

Loving Easter Greetings

1. TUCK ARTISTIC SERIES CIRCA 1906. UNLIKE SCHONIAN'S DWARVES THIS DWARF SEEMS TERRIFIED BY THE RABBIT WHO LOOKS LIKE HE IS GUARDING THE EGGS RATHER THEN CONTEMPLATING THEIR DISTRIBUTION. ★★ 2. NASH CARD E 37 SHOWS A RABBIT PLAYING THE GAME DIABLO WITH A PRETTY COLORED EASTER EGG. IN 1914, WHEN THIS CARD WAS SENT, DIABLO WAS A FAVORITE AND INEXPENSIVE GAME TO BE PLAYED BY CHILDREN, ADULTS, AND IT SEEMS, RABBITS TOO. ★

1. NASH E-40. HAPPY, PLEASANT-LOOKING CHILDREN WERE POPULAR SUBJECTS. WELL-BEHAVED, "NICE" CHILDREN WERE WHAT PEOPLE EXPECTED AND WANTED. THIS SWEET LITTLE GIRL WAS TYPICAL OF HOW CHILDREN WERE ENVISIONED. ★   2. WHITNEY POSTCARD 1914. THE PERFECT COUPLE DRESSED IN THEIR EASTER BEST GO STEPPING OUT AMIDST THE YELLOW AND PURPLE HYACINTHS. ★

Easter Greetings

GERMAN AMERICAN ART PUBLISHING
CARDS FROM TSN SERIES 555 SIGNED BY
ARTIST ALF SCHONIAN.

THE NATURAL PERFECTION OF THE BACKGROUND
GIVES CREEDENCE TO THE EXISTENCE OF THE
DWARFS AND THE PHENOMENA OF THEIR WORLD.
EVEN THEY MAY WONDER ABOUT RABBITS THAT
HATCH FROM SUPER EGGS. ★★★ EACH

Easter Greetings

1

I. THIS 1905 NOVELTY CARD IS SHEER FANTASY ON
AN EMBOSSED CARD WITH METALLIC PAINT AND
GOLD ENHANCING ★   2. THIS 1909 GERMAN
PRINTED GREETING WOULD STARTLE ANY MOTHER
HEN. WITH MONOCLE, TOP HAT, WALKING STICK
AND CIGARETTE HOLDER, THIS LITTLE BOY LOOKS
MORE LIKE HE SHOULD BE ON A NEW YEARS CARD
RATHER THAN POPPING OUT OF AN EASTER EGG!
ONE OF THE FEW EASTER-LOOKING ASPECTS OF
THIS CARD IS THE PUSSY WILLOW, A HARBINGER
OF SPRING. ★

2

A HAPPY EASTER

THIS IS A BEAUTIFULLY EMBOSSED AND GOLD
EMBELLISHED FANTASY CARD OF A RABBIT FAMILY
COMING TO VISIT AND DELIVER THE BOUNTY OF
THE HOLIDAY TO A RED CLAD GNOME. HIS HOME
IS MADE OF A LARGE EGG COVERED WITH DAISIES
AND FOUR-LEAF CLOVERS. HE IS ONE OF THE
GUARDIANS OF FIELD AND FOREST. ★★

1. AN INTERESTING USE OF A NURSERY RHYME AND
ANTHROPOMORPHISM. A LITTLE BO PEEP RABBIT IS
OUT WALKING HER SHEEP AND FINDS BRIGHTLY
COLORED EASTER EGGS. ★★   2. SERIES 809. NICELY
EMBOSSED AND GOLD ENHANCED, THE RABBIT IS A
SYMBOL OF FERTILITY AND THE LILY IS PURITY. ★★

Walpurgis- nacht

On the Eve of May Day.

UNLIKE EASTER witches, those that congregate on May Day eve usually run about scantily clad or even naked. They gather on Mount Brocken where they dance and eat while the devil fiddles. Bram Stoker's novel *Dracula* begins on Walpurgis when the vampires and undead roam and terrorize the living. The card art done for Walpurgis is often exceptional but only a small amount of cards were produced. Hold-to-lights, nudes, and mechanicals sporting superior graphics as well as beautiful lithography make this a highly competitive category for collectors. These cards tend to be dark and ominous like a storm, but those with beautiful young naked witches are not. Mount Brocken is a tourist place for mountain climbers and serious hikers to scale most of the year and there is a large building on its flat peak that welcomes visitors who arrive on foot or broomstick. Brocken is the home of many legends about demons and devils but hikers claim to find only fresh air and beautiful scenery there.

On Walpurgis night the common people gathered elder leaves and affixed them to their windows and doors to stop witches charms. Garlic was another good way to keep them away, however, we do not recommend this as it may keep ones friends and associates away also. Many fairy tales and legends take place on this night.

1. AUTOCHROME CARD 3393. WHAT FUN IT IS TO GET ON YOUR BROOM AND FLY OFF TO THE MOUNTAIN BROCKEN ON THIS NIGHT. ORACULAR, THE NOVEL, BEGINS ON WALPURGISNACHT AND IT WAS A NIGHT WHEN THE VAMPIRES AND OTHER EVIL AND UNDEAD CREATURES ROAMED THE EARTH. THIS IS A RATHER COMIC RENDITION. ★★★
2. GEBRUDER JANECKE, HANNOVER. WITCHES, BEAUTIFUL AND UGLY, NOT ONLY RODE ON BROOMS, BUT ALSO OFTEN GOATS AND PIGS. THE MOUNTAIN BROCKEN HAS MANY ELECTRICAL STORMS WHICH SEEM TO ADD TO THE GAIETY OF THIS PARTY. ★★★

Die Glücks Hexe!

wenden

AR & C, IB. NO. 825

LITTLE WITCH BY J. JAHL. WHO COULD NOT BE
BEWITCHED BY THIS SWEET LITTLE HEXEN? ★★★

WASHINGTON TAKING LEAVE OF HIS OFFICERS.

Patriotic

BECAUSE THERE are so many patriotic holidays and because the patriotic theme even flows into other holidays, we have tried to give an overall view showing ones that have major similarities in motif and those that have very little in common. Washington and Lincoln's birthday, Independence Day, and Memorial Day are those that have the most representation.

For many years, Washington's birthday was observed on February 22. (Today, it is combined with that of Lincoln and all the other presidents and called Presidents' Day.) Scenes of the Revolutionary War, the cherry tree episode, the Continental

TUCK'S SERIES 156.

WASHINGTON TAKING LEAVE OF HIS OFFICERS. ★

"Yet who would hold his dearest back,
And who would count his loss but gain"

IN MEMORY OF OUR HEROES

MEMORIAL DAY

Chapman

①

1. INTERNATIONAL ARTS SIGNED BY ARTIST CHAPMAN. MEMORIAL DAY WITH LADY LIBERTY HOLDING OUT THE LAUREL CROWN IN ONE HAND WITH THE FLAG CRADLED AGAINST HER. IN THE DISTANCE, THE LEGIONS OF THE FALLEN MARCH ON. ★★ 2. THERE ARE VERY FEW CARDS SHOWING THOMAS JEFFERSON, THE AUTHOR OF THE DECLARATION OF INDEPENDENCE AND PRESIDENT OF THE UNITED STATES. ★★

Congress, the first flag, the first swearing in of the President, and his Masonic Lodge are just some of the images that were produced. George and his hatchet with the cherry tree and George on his white stallion seem to appear in more variations than any others. On the whole, they are well-designed and very colorful.

Thomas Jefferson, on the other hand, is rarely found on cards even if he is one of

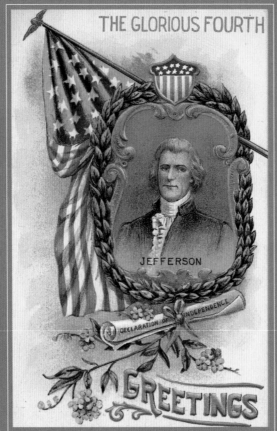

THE GLORIOUS FOURTH

JEFFERSON

DECLARATION OF INDEPENDENCE

GREETINGS

②

the most important figures in the early history of the United States.

Independence Day cards, often with fireworks depicted on them, have found a market outside of postcard collectors and, hence, the price is at a premium.

Abraham Lincoln is very popular with Civil War buffs and also because he was a romantic figure in the sense that his life and death read like a hero from a romance novel.

Memorial Day often show images of the Grand Army of the Republic veterans. Only a few exist that show Confederate soldiers, but occasionally we see veterans of both armies on a single card. Both Lincoln and Civil War collectors seek these Memorial Day cards as well. Because they are so colorful and nicely embossed and the subject matter is one that fascinates so many, these two holidays have an avid following. Lincoln cards can also be found filed under Black America.

Red, white, and blue dominate patriotic cards. The American flag in its various stages (13 stars on up), Miss Liberty, Laurel wreaths, Uncle Sam, the bald eagle, Columbia, the Statue of Liberty, fireworks, the rose—representing the northern states, and the lily—representing the southern states, are reoccurring images for these holidays but no one image occurs on all of them except the flag.

Patriotism is not just an American institution but one practiced by the natives of all countries and, therefore, it is not unusual to see patriotic cards from other countries. During wartime there is usually a flare of patriotism, which either embellishes the anger at ones enemies or makes it easier to cope with the horrible task at hand. Humor is often included, if for no other reason, to release tension. During World War I British artists had a grand time making fun of Kaiser Bill. During World War II Hitler and his pals were seen looking out of toilet

bowls, behind bars, lynched from a tree, and decorating garbage cans. These images usually fall under the category of propaganda so we have not included many of them in this book. In some cases, they became incorporated into a holiday so you might find them sprinkled into areas like Christmas. Because a country is "the enemy" at any given time does not mean that they do not feel patriotic about their country and, again, sprinklings of these may be found in this book if they were included in the celebration of any particular holiday.

1. DECORATION DAY SERIES # 1. CIVIL WAR VETERAN TAKING HIS HAT OFF IN HONOR OF THOSE THAT FELL ON BOTH SIDES OF THE WAR. ★ 2. DECORATION DAY SERIES #150. SOLDIERS OF ALL PERIODS FROM ALL BRANCHES OF THE ARMED FORCES MARCH TOGETHER. ★

INDEPENDENCE DAY SERIES 109 BY TUCK

1. FIREWORKS ARE THE MOST DANGEROUS, MOST LOOKED-FORWARD
TO, AND COLORFUL PART OF THIS DAY. ★★   2.FIREWORKS RECREATE
THE SCENE THAT FRANCIS SCOTT KEY SAW WHEN HE WROTE THE
"STAR SPANGLED BANNER." IT IS A VERY IMPORTANT PART OF THE
CELEBRATING AS THIS LITTLE BOY IN A SAILOR SUIT SHOWS. ★

1. SERIES NO. 1 NO. 1095. COMIC RENDITION OF BAD
LOGIC. A BOY WON'T GET KILLED WITH FIREWORKS
ON THE 4TH IF HIS PARENTS KILL HIM THEMSELVES
ON THE 3RD. ★   2. SERIES # 22–110 SIGNED BY
ARTIST L PELTIER. PATRIOTISM IS NOT SOLELY AN
AMERICAN INSTITUTION. HERE IS A FRENCH PATRIOTIC
CARD, PERHAPS, FOR BASTILLE DAY! AFTER THE
NAUGHTY VISUAL PUN IS DIGESTED WE WILL REVEAL
THAT WE SLIPPED THIS IN AND IT IS REALLY FOR
EASTER. PATRIOTISM IS UTILIZED DIFFERENTLY IN
DIFFERENT COUNTRIES. ★★★

1. INTERNATIONAL ART NO. 2444 BY ARTIST ELLEN CLAPSADDLE. CLAPSADDLE'S LITTLE BOY IN A CIVIL WAR UNIFORM IS TYPICAL OF THE IDEALIZED ROMANTICIZED VISION OF PATRIOTISM THAT WAS PREVELENT IN 1900–1920. ★   2. A LITTLE BOY DRESSED AS UNCLE SAM CELEBRATES THE 4TH OF JULY WITH FIREWORKS. ★

DECORATION DAY SERIES NO. 3.

THE BADGE OF THE GRAND ARMY OF THE REPUBLIC AND
A MEDAL OF THE WAR YEARS ARE INTERTWINED WITH
THE FLAG, ROSES THAT SYMBOLIZED THE NORTH, THE
EAGLE AND THE LAUREL LEAF, WERE REMINDERS THAT
THERE WERE STILL CIVIL WAR VETERANS ALIVE. THE
MEDALS ARE NICELY ENHANCED WITH SILVER. ★

2. 1776 TO 1900 THE SOLDIERS IN THEIR UNIFORMS ARE
SHOWN WITH BOTH THE FLAG THEY FOUGHT UNDER AND
THE LAUREL WREATH THEY WON. ★

1. NASH DECORATION DAY SERIES NO. 3. ROSES TO BE LAID ON THE TOMBS OF FALLEN HEROS. ★ 2. A LITTLE BOY WITH HIS GRANDMOTHER RECOLLECT AND RELIVE THE EVENTS OF THE CIVIL WAR. THE CHILD IS WEARING HIS GRANDFATHER'S BADGE, HAT, AND SWORD. ★

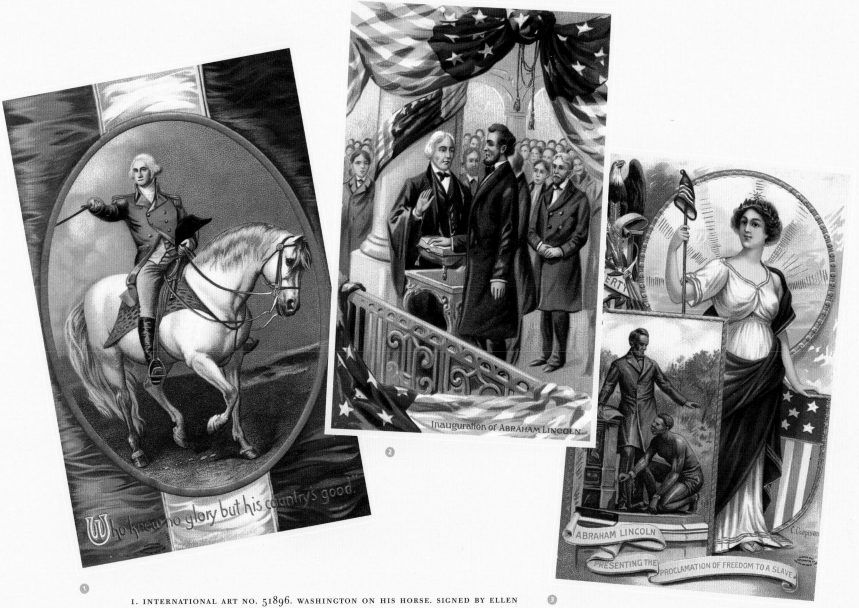

1. INTERNATIONAL ART NO. 51896. WASHINGTON ON HIS HORSE. SIGNED BY ELLEN CLAPSADDLE. ★   2. NASH SERIES NO. 1. LINCOLN CENTENNIAL SOUVENIR 1909 THE EMANCIPATING OF THE SLAVES. ★★   3. INTERNATIONAL ART NO. 51658 SIGNED BY CHAPMAN. LIBERTY AND THE SYMBOLS OF FREEDOM ABOUND. A VIGNETTE OF LINCOLN PRESENTING THE EMANCIPATION PROCLAMATION. ★★

1. E. SANDEN A PORTRAIT OF LINCOLN AND A PEEK INTO THE THEATER BOX AS LINCOLN WAS SHOT. ★★ 2. NASH SERIES NO. 1. LINCOLN'S BIRTHDAY 1908. ★★

1. 4TH OF JULY SERIES NO. 4. CHILDREN ENJOYING FIREWORKS ★★
2. UNCLE SAM AND MISS LIBERTY STROLLING ARM AND ARM. BY ELLEN
CLAPSADDLE. ★   3. GOTTSCHAULK & DREYFUSS SERIES 2172. EVERY
SYMBOL IMAGINABLE IS ON THIS CARD; UNCLE SAM, THE STATUE OF
LIBERTY, THE AMERICAN FLAG, LAUREL WREATHS OF VICTORY,
FIREWORKS, THE EAGLE, THE WHITE HOUSE, BAGS OF THE ALMIGHTY
DOLLAR, AND MORE. ★★

1. SERIES 746 PRINTED IN SAXONY. PARADES
AND FIREWORKS ARE THE ORDER OF THE DAY. ★
2. THIS CUTE LITTLE GIRL PROVES THAT
CELEBRATING THE 4TH WITH FIREWORKS ISN'T
JUST FOR THE BOYS! ★

"Service shall with steeled sinews toil.
And labour will refresh itself with hope"

"Labor conquers everything"
"The strictest law oft becomes the severest injustice."

Halloween

WE CAN safely call October 31 the most exciting and colorful fantasy holiday of the year and probably the most expensive to collect. Orange and black are often referred to as its dominant colors because of the orange Jack-o-Lantern and the black of the night. Any autumn color with orange is a

Halloween color but green is also predominant because of the stem of the pumpkin and the fact that it begins life not orange but green. Tree leaves turn from green to gold, red, or orange. So what color is autumn? Whatever color it is, *that* is the color of Halloween.

The Jack-o-Lantern might be king that

But the images of witches, laughing moon faces, owls, Entish trees, and Vegetable People vie with one another to captivate the imagination. Of all the holidays, Halloween has some of the most astounding graphics. This may account for the fact that it is so avidly collected. The images we have chosen range from the extremely rare to ones that are highly desirable but easier to find. This is due to the fact of the vast number of collectors that find them so irresistible. Competition is fierce in this category. Some of the best artists of the day produced Halloween cards and it is quite evident when one is fortunate to see a large collection. Many artists signed their names but some of the best didn't. Publisher John Winsch's artist, Samuel Schmucker, whose bewitching women are the crème de la crème of Halloween glamour cards, never signed his artwork on the Halloween cards.

The Vegetable People are probably the essence of Halloween as they are a conglomeration of different fruits and vegetables integrated and uniquely individualistic. They dance, cavort, flirt, fall in love, chase children, smoke cigars, eat cake, and scamper about like pixies. They burrow deeply into our ancient subconscious making us

On Hallowe'en the witches resort
To test lovers hearts in a glass retort
If they turn Black she knows what to do
Should it stay Red your lover is true
Throw ink down her well, to break the charm
And your lover is safe for it will shield him from harm.

WITCH AT WORK IN HER LABORATORY, THE

On Halloween, when the hour is right
Let the witch mix a charm in a Pumpkin bright
Then rub this nearest to the heart
And the One who'll tarry you'll surely marry
If you acted right your part

want to believe they once existed and still do. They are what make the gardens and farms prosper and provide us with the sustenance that keeps us alive.

The witch, on the other hand, has many persona: she is good, she is bad, she is pretty, she is ugly, she is old, she is young, her powers are real, she is make-believe, or just a child in a costume. Never on postcards is it ever even hinted that the witches shown are more than mythical made-up beings or costumed people.

The religion Wicca, or craft of the wise, is never ridiculed nor does it have anything to do with Halloween, an American holiday, which is secular to most celebrants. As Easter and Christmas images and symbols are borrowed from all the old religions, so were they borrowed for Halloween. Wiccans do not fly through the air, cast evil spells, turn milk sour, make horses go lame, turn into rabbits, or any of the silly and intolerant charges that have been attributed to them. They are the same as everyone of any other religion.

The witches we see on postcards are purely fabricated beings as are those in fairy tales. Having separated the real from the make believe, we can concentrate on the

Ho! For a Happy Hallow E'en.

HALLO E'EN.

SH! GHOSTS!

1. BARTON & SPOONER SERIES 7107 NO. B. THE
DIAMOND JIM BRODY OF THE INSECT WORLD! ★★★
2. AMERICAN POST CARD SERIES NO. 193. SIGNED
BERNHARD WALL. ★★

faux witch which is so delightfully portrayed on Halloween postcards. Thankfully, on postcards she does not have the green skin or warts that have been boringly bestowed on her for the past half-century. The sexy or pretty witch is so much more alluring and the happy-go-lucky witch that dances with cats or flies through the air on an ear of corn, has a face and a persona that is so much more fun. Perhaps this is why these images are so predominant on Halloween postcards and the scary witch isn't. In the end, all you need to know is which witch is which.

Anthropomorphism reins on Halloween. Human attributes are given to trees, pumpkins, vegetables, automobiles, houses, and anything else that the artist could give a personality to. The artist, like a wizard with a wand, taps an inanimate object and it begins to speak and act with all the foibles of a human. Magic, mystery, and fantasy are the rule not the exception.

Charms and customs abound and some of them are very quaint. In Wales, a girl on Halloween places a knife amongst the leeks in the garden. She must do this walking backwards. Her future husband will come

1. THIS CAT COACHMAN WILL NOT BE TRAVELING VERY FAR WITH SUCH SORRY LOOKING STEEDS, INDEED. ★★ 2. RARE MAROON BORDER ON A WINSCH HALLOWEEN. ★★★★★★

and throw the knife into the middle of the garden. Hardly romantic. The girl walking backwards down the stairs with a mirror and a candle to see her true love seems a trifle more romantic but just as dangerous. Throwing an apple peel over her shoulder which will land in the shape of her true loves initial seems a lot easier and safer. There are all kinds of ways to find out whom your love will be if you will read the cards and follow suit.

The Scottish motifs show up because the poet Robert Burns is the father of this holiday. His poems, "Tam O Shanter" and "Halloween" were brought to America by Scottish (Celts) emigrants and they are the seeds that, when planted in the fertile soil of a young country, evolved into an American holiday, Halloween. These are the earliest records of the traditions and folklore that exist. As there are only modern ones for Ireland, one must accept the fact that the Celtic people that first began and brought over the holiday are Scots, not Irish, as so many people would like to believe. Burns was passing on local folklore to those of his generation and, thus, he is also the historian to whom we must bow.

A HALLOWE'EN WISH

ON HALLOWE'EN YOUR SLIGHTEST WISH IS LIKELY TO COME TRUE, SO BE CAREFUL, OR THE GOBELINS WILL SPOIL YOUR WISH FOR YOU.

DESIGN COPYRIGHTED, JOHN WINSCH, 1912.

The thistle, the tartan, the bagpipe, and kilt are often seen symbols, never the shamrock or the leprechaun.

The harvest table and those places where fortunes are told are lionized on the postcard. It was extremely important to find out who your mate was to be and all the traditions and games played were to either accomplish this or contriving to get the two people together. Saint Matrimony is, after all, the Patron Saint of Halloween, which makes this holiday a little like Valentine's Day! The bounty of the Halloween feast: pies, corn, nuts, apples, etc., are all part of the cornucopia of the Harvest festival, which we will see again in Thanksgiving and Christmas.

1. THIS SCHMUCKER CLOWN HAS A BEWITCHING (NOT A FUNNY) FACE. SITTING AMONG THE OWLS ON A TREE BRANCH SHE SENDS A POEM ABOUT A "MUMMER'S SUIT." MORRIS DANCING BY THE MUMMERS IS AN OLD ESTABLISHED TRADITION GOING BACK TO ROMAN TIMES AND EARLIER.

★★★★★ 2. WINSCH PUBLISHING SCHMUCKER

SERIES 1256 SIGNED BY ARTIST
ELLEN CLAPSADDLE.

THREE OUT OF FOUR MECHANICALS WITH MOVING ARMS,

IS PERHAPS THE MOST DESIRABLE OF ALL HALLOWEEN

CARDS. ★★★★★★★ EACH. THE BLACK CHILD IS ★★★★★★★★

1. A. HEINMÜLLER'S CHILD-WITCH WITH EVERY-
THING SHE NEEDS TO CELEBRATE HALLOWEEN
NIGHT. ★★★   2. SIGNED BERNHARDT WALL.
LITTLE WITCH WITH HER JACK-O-LANTERN. ★★

FLORENCE BAMBERGER'S HALLOWEEN DON'TS
SERIES

1–2. CIRCA 1913 BAMBERGER'S HALLOWEEN DON'TS
SERIES IS HEAVILY EMBOSSED AND COMES IN TWO
WAYS, WITH SILVER OR GOLD ENHANCEMENT. ★★ EACH

STECKER SERIES 408

1–3. THREE OF A SET OF SIX HIGHLY-EMBOSSED
CARDS OF A CLOWN CELEBRATING THE HOLIDAY IN
HIGH STYLE! ★★★ EACH

BAMBERGER SET 116

HALLOWEEN ART WAS NOT MACABRE OR SCARY. ITS FOCUS
WAS ON FUN, FANTASY, AND FROLIC. SMILING FACES,
ASTONISHED FACES, FUNNY FACES, AND CHARACTER FACES
ADD TO THE DELIGHT OF THE NIGHT. ★★★ EACH

Make a ring of pumpkin seeds
An odd old-fashioned charm,
Makes the goblins howl with fear
And keeps you safe from harm.

NASH H-12 SET OF 6 CARDS.

1–4. THIS IS A WONDERFUL FANTASY SET SHOWING
THE TWO NATURES OF WITCHES, THE GODDESS
AND THE HAG. THE BEAUTIFUL YOUNG WOMAN,
BEGUILING AND BEWITCHING THE YOUNG MAN OF
HER CHOICE, WHILE THE OLD WITCH CASTS
DIFFERENT TYPES OF SPELLS AND SOMETIMES
CAUSES MISCHIEF. ★★★ EACH

Be careful men, on Halloween
Witches inveigle and entice
Bachelors to the golden dance
That's naughty, though its nice.

If you wish to keep the witches out
And be safe on old Hallowe'en,
Draw a double cross upon the sill
Where it surely will be seen.

Halloween

Halloween

A very good scheme on old Hallowe'en,
The finish of which is easily seen.
One bewitching miss one bewitching kiss
And one good tight hug to complete your bliss

H-12

3

4

NASH SET H-25

1–3. BLACK BACKGROUND, HEAVILY EMBOSSED.
THE DIFFERENCE BETWEEN A WITCH AND A
SCIENTIST OR ALCHEMIST IS A VERY FINE
LINE! ★★ EACH

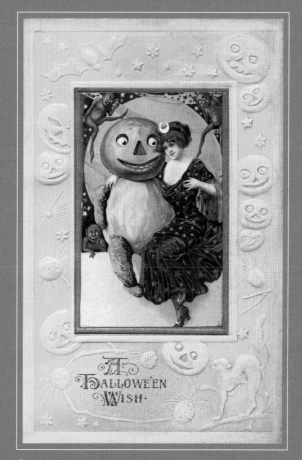

②

TWO WINSCH PUBLISHING CARDS WITH THE SAME

HIGHLY-EMBOSSED BORDER FROM A SCARCE

SERIES. THE SCHMUCKER GIRL IS EXACTLY THE

SAME IN BOTH CARDS ONLY DRESSED DIFFERENTLY.

★★★★★★ EACH

1. WINSCH PUBLISHING. BY ARTIST SAMUEL SCHMUCKER. BEAUTY ASLEEP AND DREAMING OF HER TRUE LOVE IS PROTECTED BY THE FAIRIES. ★★★★★ 2. CLAPSADDLE CHILD PLACES A JACK-O-LANTERN ON A TRI-LEGGED STOOL. ★★

HALLOWE'EN TIME

Tonight, upon your pillow,
Close your eyes and hide your head,
For the fairies and the goblins
Will be hovering round your bed.

1

A MERRY HALLOWE'EN

2

This is the night of
Hallowe'en
When all the witches
may be seen.

1. HIGHLY EMBOSSED CARD OF A CLASSICAL WITCH
IN THE SKY. PRINTED IN GERMANY. ★★★
2. OLD MR. MOON IS ENJOYING THE CHARMING
SIGHT HE SEES THIS NIGHT! ★★

1. THE WITCH AND HER CAT KNOW THIS CAR OF
THE PAST IS A LONG WAY IN THE FUTURE! ★★★
2. BERNHARDT WALL IS PROBABLY THE ARTIST FOR
THIS CARD. ★★

VALENTINE & SONS PUBLISHING, U.K.

1–2. THE JOYFUL WHIMSY OF THESE CARDS SETS
THE MOOD FOR THIS HOLIDAY. ★★★ EACH

1–3. BAMBERGER HALLOWEEN GREETINGS SET
IS ONE WHERE THE UNKNOWN ARTIST LET HIS
FANTASY RUN AWAY WITH HIM. ★★★ EACH

The Mexican Day of the Dead

DANCING SKELETONS, feasts, and singing at the candlelit graves of ones ancestors makes this one of the most charming holidays ever. It is unfortunate that there are so few cards made for this important holiday. Tin and papier-mache figures of skeletons dressed in sombreros and ponchos dancing and singing are everywhere during this feast and yet so few cards were made. Because Halloween influences this holiday and Halloween is in turn influenced by it, we found it impossible not to include a few cards. This Mexican festival in honor of their ancestors has spread across the border to California and Texas and slowly is making its way into the states.

Dark chocolate coffins with white choco-

FROM A FRESCO BY DIEGO RIVERA ★

NOCHE DE MUERTOS
JANITZIO MICH

REAL PHOTO OF PEOPLE CELEBRATING AT THE
GRAVES OF THEIR ANCESTORS ON THIS MOST
IMPORTANT OF MEXICAN HOLIDAYS. ★

late skeletons reposing under a moveable lid are just one of the tasty confections that are made for the celebrators. Mariachi bands in colorful local garb serenade the keepers of the nightlong vigil. Osmosis is taking place on both sides of the border as Halloween adopts some of the Mexican celebration and Dios Los Muertos absorbs some of Halloweens. Both have their scary side, their macabre twist, and their fun fantasy side.

As the most important Mexican artist, Diego Rivera's painting uses the colors of the desert and the essence of the country itself and when the candle smoke has

cleared the images are as striking and vibrant as an autumn day in New England as well as having political and social significance.

Giving homage to one's ancestors and placating the dead has its roots in many religions. The Armenians, even to this day, take picnics to the cemetery on Easter and share their meal with their ancestors. As this author is often in transit on Easter Sunday I have made it a tradition to stop at a cemetery, any cemetery, and place sweet buns on graves requesting those that repose there pass the prayers and messages on for us. Last year we even put marshmallow bunnies on the children's graves. And so the tradition changes and grows. We enjoyed a picnic in a serene setting and the birds have sweet fresh rolls to celebrate the day. One can only assume the ants ate the bunnies! This is how any ethnic group adds to a holiday and injects its customs on the whole. Just as I, who am not Swedish, add a few small kitchen witches to my Easter egg tree, so has the Mexican holiday been adopted by many who find that spending a moment of time, other than on Memorial Day, to honor ones ancestors and loved ones who have passed on is a comforting and rewarding experience. Besides, this is such a colorful and musical holiday that people are naturally attracted to it!

Guy Fawkes Day

"Remember, remember the fifth of November
Gunpowder Treason and Plot"

THIS HOLIDAY celebrated in England is a patriotic one. It has absolutely no connection to Halloween as has been written in the past decade. In 1605, Parliament was held on November 5th because the plague had been raging and, therefore, the reconvening had been put off quite a few times so as not to endanger the King or the members of that august body. Guy Fawkes and his fellow conspirators had planned to overthrow the government and place a different monarch on the throne, one who would be the Catholic minority or

MADAME TUSSARDS & SONS NO. 50,041.
CONSIDERING THE HISTORICAL IMPORTANCE OF THIS HOLIDAY TO THE ENGLISH, IT IS SURPRISING THAT THERE ARE SO FEW CARDS FOR THE HOLIDAY. ONE WOULD AT LEAST EXPECT MYRIADS OF FIREWORKS AND EFFIGY BURNING ON CARDS. ★

THE DISCOVERY OF GUY FAWKES.

PUBLISHED BY CASWELL & BOWDEN, LTD., BIRMINGHAM.

Hudson & Son, Lith., Birmingham.   Copyright.   Entered Stationers' Hall.

preferably a Catholic. James the 1st of England was certainly more tolerant than Elizabeth I but really cracked down after this attempt to assassinate him and his family. Fawkes was tortured, hung, drawn, and quartered and his head was left on a spike on the gates for the crows and to warn others not to even think of Regicide. The day is celebrated each year with burning Fawkes in effigy and shooting off fireworks. The confusion may have come about when an author didn't do their research and added two and two together and came up with three. The fact that masks were worn of Guy or "the Guy" as the British refer to Fawkes, or that children begged for a penny to buy fireworks does not connect it to Halloween in the least. The fireworks were in lieu of the gunpowder, which Guy Fawkes and his friends planned on using to blow up the building where the King was to open Parliament. The gunpowder had been replaced once before as it had gone bad. When Fawkes was caught in the act, it had already gone bad again and would not have ignited. Even with all the work and plotting, the plan would not have worked anyway. There are a few good scholarly studies of this period of English history and none of them confuse this day (which the British feel their form of government was preserved) with Halloween. Now that this modern day urban legend has been dispelled we hope everyone will see it as a patriotic holiday, not as an extension of Halloween. This day stands on its own, independent of any other holiday. Cards for Guy Fawkes are scarce.

MAY YOU HAVE
PEACE AND PLENTY
ON YOUR
THANKSGIVING DAY

Thanksgiving

I**N THE** days of Socrates and Plato, the Greek Gods ruled the elements. Demeter, the Goddess of the harvest, would sprinkle the contents of her cornucopia across the land and the harvest would be abundant.

The Roman goddess Pomona would perform the same function. It is not sur-prising then that the cornucopia, which held the success of the harvest, was incorporated into our Thanksgiving tradition. The Canadians also celebrate Thanksgiving in October, not in November, as here in the states. Both countries rely heavily on the agricultural segment of their economy. The cornucopia filled with fruits and vegetables

TUCK NO. 175

A FARMYARD SCENE WHICH REPRESENTS THE WISH
FOR PEACE AND PLENTY. ★

May the season of plenty bring
To you, every good thing.

THANKSGIVING GREETINGS

①

represents wealth and prosperity. Until the invention of the refrigerator and transportation systems the success of the harvest was the difference between surviving the winter or not. The fruits, nuts, berries, and vegetables along with the cornucopia were shown in abundance to wish others prosperity and to show ones own prosperity. Colorful as this produce was, the addition of a wild turkey to the picture made it even more so.

Benjamin Franklin wanted the turkey to be the national bird but John Adams wanted the bald eagle. Interestingly, the two show up (birds, not patriots) together on Thanksgiving cards adding a patriotic feel to the holiday.

Thanksgiving is also associated with peace as it goes hand in hand with prosperity. One seldom can have one without the other.

The brave Indian men and the beautiful Indian maidens bringing pumpkin pies, turkey, and venison to the Pilgrims—that is how we wish to believe the first Thanksgiving was celebrated—with everyone living in friendship and harmony. The Pilgrim men are rugged and godly and the women and children were their equals. Fortunately, the myth is much prettier and more palatable than the truth, which means we have some beautiful cards of the first Thanksgiving.

GIBSON PUBLISHING. THE GODDESS OF THE HARVEST SPRINKLES PLENTY FROM HER CORNUCOPIA. ★

Samuel Schmucker's Pilgrim women and Indian maidens are outstanding.

Harvest scenes and comic cards centering on either the killing of the turkey or the turkey's thoughts about the holiday are some of the best. Not only are they very colorful and fanciful, but also they add lightness to a holiday that has sometimes been steeped in a misdirected sobriety. Turkeys driving corncob cars with their bonneted mate beside them are the opposite side of the story—Thanksgiving as the turkey would like it to be.

The use of the pumpkin in its evolved form, the Jack-o-Lantern, are important because the pumpkin isn't just something to make into a pumpkin pie. The philosophy that Halloween is to Thanksgiving what Santa is to Christmas comes into play here. The Victorians were rather straight-laced and stuffy, though nowhere as bad as the Puritans. With the coming of the Edwardian era, everyone loosened their stays and the literary and artistic freedom that ensued is why postcard art is so refreshing. Children are allowed to be children and that rare bird that wants to hop on a train and get away from the November stress is able to do so.

1. TUCK SERIES 162. NO MATTER HOW DIFFERENT, WHERE CAN THIS TURKEY GO ON THANKSGIVING DAY THAT HE WILL BE SAFE? ★   2. AN EARLY AIRPLANE IN PURSUIT OF AN AIRBORNE TURKEY. ★

Thanksgiving Day

"BOYS, I FEEL I'M GOING TO A CHANGE OF CLIMATE."

THANKSGIVING GREETINGS

Thanksgivings Greetings.

DESIGN COPYRIGHTED JOHN WINSCH. 1914.

HEARTY THANKSGIVING GREETING

DESIGN COPYRIGHTED, JOHN WINSCH, 1912.

1. INDIAN WOMAN AT A CAMPFIRE PREPARING FOR THE FEAST AS A BRAVE APPROACHES WITH THE PIECE-DE-RESISTANCE, THE TURKEY. ★★★ 2. WINSCH PUBLISHING 1912 BY ARTIST SAMUEL SCHMUCKER. THE EASE WITH WHICH THE INDIAN MAIDEN HOLDS THE LARGE TURKEY IS AMAZING. TWO BEAUTIFUL WOMEN OF TWO DIFFERENT RACES. ★★★

JOHN WINSCH PUBLISHING 1911

1. IS THE TURKEY FOLLOWING THE WOMAN BECAUSE OF THE APPLES IN HER APRON OR

BECAUSE SHE IS A SCHMUCKER CREATION? ★★★ 2. SCHMUCKER'S BEAUTIFUL WOMAN HAS

LED THE TURKEY INTO THE HOUSE AND HIS PROVERBIAL GOOSE HAS BEEN COOKED! DINNER

IS BEING SERVED IN THE MAIN DINING ROOM BON APPETITE! ★★★   3. JOHN WINCH

PUBLISHING 1911. THE GOLDEN SUN ACTS AS A HALO ON THE SCHMUCKER FARM GIRL. ★★

Greeting Thanksgiving

Thanksgiving Greetings

Thanksgiving Day

1. NASH SERIES T26. A TURKEY WITH PERSONA. ★★   2. A&S PUBLISH-
ING. UNCLE SAM, AS PROUD AS A TURKEY, STRUTTING ON HIS DAY. ★★
3. GIBSON 1910 A. VON BEUST NO. 131. THERE IS A HAPPY-JOYFUL
QUALITY ABOUT THIS CARD WHICH TO AN AGRARIAN SOCIETY MEANT A
SUCCESSFUL HARVEST IN AND A TIME TO RELAX A BIT AND VISIT IN
THE WARMTH OF A HOME WITH WELL-STOCKED LARDER. ★

1. TUCK NO. 175. A LOVELY WAY TO SPEND THANKSGIVING DAY, RIDING ALONG IN A CORN COB CAR AND ENJOYING THE AUTUMN COLORS. ★★
2. TUCK NO. 123. SAFE FOR ANOTHER YEAR, THIS COUPLE SPENDS THE DAY MOTORING. ★★
3. A TURKEY TROTTER AS OPPOSED TO A TURKEY TREAT! ★

Thanksgiving Greetings

MAY YOU BE
THANKFUL
ALSO TURKFUL

1. THIS GERMAN-MADE CARD HAS THE SWEET-CHEEKED CHILDREN FATTENING UP THE HOLIDAY TURKEY. ★★   2. WHITNEY MADE, PREPARING FOR THANKSGIVING IS HARD WORK. ★

1

1. HALLOWEEN AND THANKSGIVING HAVE
MANY SIMILARITIES AND USE MANY OF THE
SAME SYMBOLS LIKE THE JACK-O-LANTERN. ★
2. MECHANICAL OF TWO TURKEYS. WHEN
THE WHEELS ARE TURNED THE TURKEY'S
FEATHERS GIVE A PINWHEEL OR
KALEIDOSCOPE EFFECT. ★★★

2

1. P. SANDER CIRCA 1908 NO. 331. THE HORN OF PLENTY FROM
THE HARVEST THAT, HOPEFULLY, GRACES EVERY HOME. ★

2. UNCLE SAM CUTS INTO A JUICY TURKEY, ONE HE WOULD HAVE
BEEN PROUD TO PUT HIS U.S. STAMP OF APPROVAL ON. ★★

3. NO. 964. A PICTURESQUE HOME PICTURE FRAMED BY A DELLA
RUBIN-TYPE WREATH AS THE FRUIT OF THE HARVEST. ★

Krampus

IN AUSTRIA on December 5, Krampus is celebrated. Men dressed as furry, black, devil-like creatures with long tongues parade out in the streets carrying birch switches. Krampus, often represented as wearing chains and accompanying St. Nicholas, is the antithesis of the saint he serves. St. Nicholas is kind and giving and gives gifts to those who have been good. An apple, a pear, a doll, a tin drum, and a Christmas tree—with all the warmth and happiness that the kind and godly deserve—are his bounty. His companion, Krampus, gets to give those who have misbehaved their just rewards. Even today, Krampus figures run about at the festival using their switch on any and all they encounter. Some that go to the Austrian Festival find it frightening and even painful if they happen

C.H.W. NO. 2503-28

KRAMPUS CATCHING HIS VICTIMS IN A SPIDER

WEB. ★★★

Er könnte Dir gefährlich sein,
Der Krampus, der im Spinnetz sitzt gefangen.
Drum solltest Du ihn nicht befrei'n,
Ersparst für Dich viel Angst und Bangen.

135

to have been unfortunate enough to have become victims of Krampus's switch. Candy containers and postcards show variations in his looks. Sometimes he is red and sometimes he is black. The earlier cards are scarier and, in the more recent ones, Krampus has been turned into a little cupid-type imp and the sexual connotation is quite obvious. The spelling can vary with the first letter being either a G or a K. Either Grampus or Krampus is acceptable.

The earliest cards are in the Gruss Aus category with Gruss Aus, meaning "Greetings From." The more gold on the card the later it is and if the card stock is heavy and all one color front and back, it is earlier.

Krampus cards warn one not to be naughty but some of them insinuate that it can be quite fun to be naughty. Sending this card to someone can either mean the sender is being rakish or giving a warning. Either way you are not going to get candy!

C.H.W. NO. 2503-3 CIRCA 1928

KRAMPUS DROPS A BAD CHILD INTO

A BUCKET. ★★★

WHEN DID Christmas really begin? Was it the moment the Christ child was born in a manger in Bethlehem? Because many of the old religions celebrated the birth of the dying god and because both the birth of Osiris and Mithras were celebrations the early Christians were aware of and frowned on, it was decided to move the date from January 6 to December 25 which is now the date most churches celebrate Christmas.

The birth of Mithras was an important event as his worshipers, who were fire worshipers, were spread over all of what is Iran and Iraq and much of Anatolia. The only way to keep the early Christians from

Christmas

participating in the celebrations was to change the date. The celebration of Christmas as we know it and celebrate it is relatively recent. The Puritans forbade its celebration because of its Pagan symbolism, and even today some denominations follow suit.

Each country has a special flavor that they inject into the celebration of a holiday with their ethnic traditions. Many of our American traditions come from Germany because of the large amount of German emigrants that settled in large pockets about the country. The Dresden ornaments, the crèche figures, and the Belschnickles, or Father Christmas figures, are just a few of the decorative items that many think are American or English in origin but were brought to America by German emigrants or were produced for their consumption after they arrived. Today these are considered treasured heirlooms. Before the days of plastic tinsel, there was real tinsel and it was sold in decorative folders for storage so that it could be used again the next year.

We could isolate each country's contri-

THIS HOLD-TO-LIGHT CARD SHOWS FATHER CHRISTMAS IN HIS GREEN ROBES TRIMMED IN BROWN FUR. THIS IS HOW MOST ENGLISH WOULD HAVE CONCEIVED THE TRADITIONAL GIFT GIVER IN 1905 WHEN THIS CARD WAS SENT. ★★★★★★★★

bution to Christmas separately but that would take away from the whole. Christmas is not the product of just one country, and as the art compliments each other as well as being distinctive; it seems appropriate to keep them together.

The star that shone over Bethlehem; the mistletoe, a magical green which represents love and healing; the holly which is the holy plant and brings protection; the Yule log, which brought warmth and heat through fire to the home; the Wassail bowl, which was cheer, goodwill, and friendship; and the gift giver who comes in many different guises, are some of the motifs you will see repeated. The giving of gifts, whether from the hands of the Magi, in the form of an angel, Father Christmas in any of his persona, dwarves or elves, all perform the same task. The giving, not the receiving, is the important component.

Each year as the prices escalate and pressure is exerted by large corporations for us to consume, it is a balm to slip back to Victorian days and recall some of the words Charles Dickens wrote in "A Christmas Carol." Scrooge's nephew, Fred, said, "There are many things which I might have derived

I. INTERNATIONAL ARTS NO. 2790 CIRCA 1910. WE JUST DON'T BUILD SNOWMEN LIKE THIS ANYMORE!

★★ 2. A MODERN DAY SANTA ARRIVING LADEN WITH PACKAGES. ★★

A MERRY Christmas.

gold or silver in my pocket, I believe that it has done me good, and will do me good; and I say, God Bless it!" This is the essence of the holiday celebration.

The essence of giving is also from Dickens. "At this time of the rolling year," the specter said, "I suffer most. Why did I walk through the crowds of fellow beings, with my eyes turned down, and never raised them to that blessed star which led the wise men to a poor abode? Were there no poor homes to which its light would have conducted me?" It was at this point in the story Marley floats back down amongst those who had lost all capability to intercede on human behalf and help those who needed it. If anything sets the secular stage for the meaning of the Christmas celebration it is within the original text of this immortal Christmas story. This and Jean Carlo Menotti's opera "Amahal and the Night Visitors" are what little is left to us of a holiday which has lost its significance to many.

Looking at the cards, both those sent and kept, we are swept back to a time less commercial and less egotistical. Christmas is dreams and visions of wonderment. These dreams and visions can be found in the images captured in postcards. A dream fulfilled is no longer a dream but reality. "And visions of sugar plums danced in their heads." Sometimes the dreams are so much better than the reality. We dream of Santa

good, by which I have not profited, I dare say, Christmas among the rest. But I am sure I have always thought of Christmas time, when it has come around—apart from the veneration due to its sacred name and origin, if anything belonged to it can be apart from that—as a good time; a kind forgiving, charitable, pleasant time; the only time I know of in the long calendar of the year, when men and women seem by one consent to open up their shut up hearts freely, and to think of people below them as if they really were fellow passengers to the grave, and not another race of creatures bound on other journeys. And, therefore, Uncle, therefore it has never put a scrap of coming at midnight and eating the cookies we left him along with the cold glass of milk. We dream of the stuffed stockings hanging in front of the fireplace when most of us don't have a fireplace. We dream of the North Pole and elves working away so that on Christmas Eve Santa and his reindeer can deliver gifts to everyone the world over, especially those who are in such desperate need. We dream of the Christmas's of our childhood and of the angel on the top of the tree that has been handed down from one generation to another. Above all, we dream of giving someone else something that will make their eyes shine brighter than the lights reflecting off the tinsel on the Christmas tree. The visions of Christmas past relived on these cards give a comforting feeling that the nostalgia of the past might come full circle with the future and become one with the present. As Tiny Tim said, " God Bless Us Everyone!"

NO. 15913

FATHER CHRISTMAS IN HIS TRADITIONAL ROBE

WITH TWO CHERUBS DELIVERING GIFTS THROUGH

A WINDOW. ★★

A Joyful Christmas.

1. PRINTED IN GERMANY. CHILDREN WATCHING FATHER CHRISTMAS OUTSIDE THEIR WINDOW. ★★ 2. SERIES I. IN COLD NORDIC COUNTRIES SANTA IS GREEN AS A VERDANT SYMBOL OF REJUVINATION. ★★ 3. BARTON AND SPOONER NO. 7157. SANTA WATCHING CHILDREN MISBEHAVING THROUGH A PEEP HOLE IN THE NORTH POLE. ★★

1. WINSCH 1911. THE TEDDY BEAR WAS BORN DURING TEDDY ROOSEVELT'S TIME AND NAMED AFTER HIM BECAUSE OF HIS REFUSAL TO KILL TWO BEAR CUBS. ★★
2. SIGNED BY ITALIAN ARTIST COLOMBO. ELEPHANT TOYS WERE STILL VERY POPULAR AS MANY REMEMBERED THE FAMOUS BARNUM ELEPHANT, JUMBO. ★★   3. GIBSON SANTA AND TOYS. IT IS INTERESTING THAT THE BORDER HAS A FEW WITCH TOYS ON IT. IN SOME COUNTRIES THE WITCH IS THE BRINGER OF GIFTS. ★★

MAY
CHRISTMAS
JOYS WITH
YOU AGREE
FROM
CHRISTMAS
WEIGHTS MAY
YOU BE FREE.

Squeeze the Card

May Good Luck
Cling to You

A Merry
Christmas

1. LEST ANYONE THINK THERE ISN'T ANY HUMOR-
OUS ARTIST SIGNED CARDS FOR THE HOLIDAYS,
HERE IS ONE OF THIS AUTHOR'S FAVORITES. ★★
2. A SQUEAKIER NOVELTY CARD PRINTED IN
GERMANY. BECAUSE CARDS LIKE THIS WERE
IMPOSSIBLE NOT TO BE PLAYED WITH, THEY WERE
OFTEN DAMAGED AND ARE DIFFICULT TO FIND
IN GOOD CONDITION. AUTOMOTIVE FAILURE
WAS A FACT OF LIFE EVEN IN THE "GOOD OLDE
DAYS". ★★★

How would you like to "cut in" to this old bird this Xmas?

1. BAMFORTH CHRISTMAS CARTOON SERIES. DURING WORLD WAR I KAISER WILLHELM OF GERMANY WAS SO DISLIKED THAT HE WAS A MAJOR CARTOON CHARACTER FOR A POPULACE THAT LOVED TO LOATH THE MAN. HE WAS CARICATURED AND LAMPOONED IN EVERY POSSIBLE WAY WITH HIS LOOKS, AFFECTATIONS AND DEFORMITY (ONE OF HIS ARMS WAS SHORTER THAN THE OTHER). THIS WAS USED TO GOOD ADVANTAGE BY POSTCARD ARTISTS. THE BRITISH HAD A GRAND OLD TIME ROASTING HIM IN EVERY WAY THEY COULD POSSIBLY CONCEIVE. ★★ 2. KAISER BILL WOULD HAVE TO STAND UNDER ITS MISTLETOE A VERY LONG TIME BEFORE HE FOUND ANYONE FOOLISH ENOUGH TO KISS HIM! ★★

Would you like to win an Iron Cross this Xmas?

1. A HOLLY CLAD CHILD IN THE ROLE OF THE GIFT GIVER, A SORT OF PAGAN PRE SANTA, EARTH GOD. WINSCH PUBLISHING 1910 ★★★ 2–3. ARCTIC EXPLORATION AND THE EXPLOITS OF PERRY AND SCOTT CAUGHT THE IMAGINATION OF THE PUBLIC. THE SNOW BABY WAS BORN OUT OF THIS POLAR FRENZY. ELLEN CLAPSADDLE'S RENDITIONS WERE EXCEEDINGLY POPULAR IN THEIR DAY. THESE CHILDREN WITH THEIR POLES OF EVERGREENS AND POINSETTIAS ARE WHIMSICAL REMINDERS OF PERPETUITY. ★★★ EACH

1. SPOONER & BARTON CHILDREN AT PLAY IN FRONT OF
THE TREE, NICELY ENHANCED WITH SILVER. ★★
2. FAMILY AROUND THE CHRISTMAS TREE THAT IS LIT
WITH REAL CANDLES. ★★   2. WINSCH PUBLISHING 1911
SCHMUCKER WOMAN WITH SNOWBALLS. SNOWBALL-
THROWING WAS A PROVOCATIVE SPORT BECAUSE IT COULD
BE INDULGED IN BY BOTH SEXES. ★★

1. EAS PUBLISHING 1909. THE ANGEL IS THE GIFT
GIVER. THE FAWN REPRESENTS INNOCENCE AND
CHILDHOOD. ★ 2. PUBLISHER EAS'S RENDITION OF
AN ANGELIC CHILD REPRESENTS HOW IMPORTANT
THE INNOCENCE OF CHILDHOOD IS TO CHRISTMAS. ★

1. ITALIAN PUBLISHER, DEGANNI, # 5048 BY
ARTIST BUSI, WHO IS ONE OF THE MOST VERSA-
TILE AND COLLECTIBLE OF THE ITALIAN ARTISTS.
THERE IS A HINT OF WHITNEY MADE'S NIMBLE
NICKS IN THESE TWO CHILDREN-ELVES. ★★★
2. WHITNEY MADE'S NIMBLE NICKS MAY HAVE
BEEN THE INSPIRATION FOR ROSE O'NEILL'S
KEWPIES. IN THEIR CUDDLY CUTE WAY THEY ARE
ACTING AS THE GIFT GIVER. ★★

1. SERIES NO. 358. DECORATING ONE'S GARMENTS WITH HOLLY MADE ONE LOOK FESTIVE. ★★ 2. TUCK #8447. BEAUTY AND LOVE KNOW NO AGE. DANCE PARTIES WERE VERY POPULAR AMUSEMENTS FOR THE HOLIDAY SEASON OF THE WEALTHY. ★★ 3. TUCK 9444. MOTHER AND DAUGHTER WORK IN THE KITCHEN MAKING THE CHRISTMAS PUDDING. ★

Buon Natale

A HAPPY CHRISTMAS

A COLD WELCOME.

1. WINSCH PUBLISHING 1910. EVEN THE SCHMUCKER WOMAN'S DRESS HAS POINSETTIAS ON IT. ★★ 2. ITALIAN ARTIST COLOMBO WAS WELL KNOWN FOR THE CONTRASTING BACKGROUND VERSUS THE COLORS WORN BY THE FIGURES. IT WAS QUITE COMMON BACK IN 1912 WHEN THIS CARD WAS DONE, TO DEPICT CHILDREN AND CHERUBS NAKED, AND NOT MINDING, THE COLD AND SNOW. ★★ 2. TUCK OILETTE 9445 CIRCA 1909. SHE IS NOT SO PRIM AND PROPER THAT SHE WON'T THROW A SNOWBALL OR TWO! ★

A merry

Christmas

to you

X. 659-4.

A happy Christmas

1. X659-4. EMBOSSED AND ENHANCED WITH SIL-
VER. FATHER CHRISTMAS KNOCKING ON THE DOOR.
★★. 2. S.P.C. LONDON NO. 284 ★★★

1. A&S #409. SANTA IN A BLUE ROBE PUSHES A
GOLDEN-ENHANCED WHEELBARROW FULL OF
HOLIDAY GREENS AND GIFTS. ★★ 2. STECKER
SERIES? SANTA WRITING IN HIS BOOK IF YOU'RE
BEEN NAUGHTY OR NICE! ★★

I. SL & CO. SILK SUITED SANTA DELIVERING A
DOLL TO A LITTLE GIRL SLEEPING UNDER A SILK
COMFORTER. ★★★ 2. TUCK OILETTE NO. 8247
SIGNED H. SANDFORD. CIRCA 1907. FATHER
CHRISTMAS PLAYS TUG-OF-WAR WITH THREE
CHILDREN USING A CHRISTMAS CRACKER. THESE
WERE VERY POPULAR IN ENGLAND, BUT SELDOM
USED IN THE STATES. INSIDE THE CRACKER WOULD
BE A SILLY HAT AND A PRIZE OR FAVOR OF SOME
KIND. ★★

1. GERMAN, EMBOSSED, AND ENHANCED WITH
GOLD. A MODERN SANTA, FOR HIS DAY, IN A BLUE
DRIVING COAT AND WEARING GOGGLES. ★★

2. P. SANDERS PUBLISHING'S SILK-SUITED SANTA,
FLIES OVER A PICTURESQUE TOWN WITH HIS
MAGICAL HOLLY WAND IN HAND AND A SLEIGH
FULL OF TOYS. THE SILK SUITED CARDS WERE ALSO
PRODUCED WITHOUT THE NOVELTY ADDITION AND
THEY WOULD HAVE BEEN LESS EXPENSIVE. ★★

Loving
Christmas Wishes

Wishing you a Merry Christmas

Christmas Greetings

1. PFB NO. TINY CHILDREN PLAYING IN
A HOLLY BUSH BRANCH. ★★   2. TUCK
SANTA CLAUS SERIES NO. 512. TWO SNOW
BABY-TYPES IN THE WOODS GATHERING
HOLLY. ★   3. TUCK NO. 512. A CHILD,
ALMOST A WOMAN, HOLDS A DOLL. ★★

1. TUCK OILETTE 9445 CIRCA 1909. SILK-SUITED SANTA SPEAKS WITH DANCING CHILDREN. ★   2. CIRCA 1907. UNDER THE CHRISTMAS TREE EVEN DOLLS CAN WOO AND FALL IN LOVE. THIS IS A TRULY MAGICAL SEASON. ★★   3. PRESIDENT TEDDY ROOSEVELT'S ENCOUNTER WITH THE TWO BEAR CUBS PRODUCED A NEW TOY, THE TEDDY BEAR. THE EARLIEST ONES LOOKED MORE LIKE REAL BEARS THAN THE ONES WE SEE TODAY. IN 1910 WHEN THIS CARD WAS SENT IT WAS EVERY CHILD'S DREAM TO HAVE ONE, THEREFORE, THE EXPRESSION ON THIS CHILD'S FACE IS NOT SURPRISING. ★

Buon Natale

A happy Christmas

A MERRY CHRISTMAS TO YOU.

1. SBORGI. MADONNA OF PEACE BY
FRA ANGELICO. HIGH EMBOSSING
WITH GOLD ENHANCING. ★★
2. BARTON & SPOONER SERIES 7055B
GELATIN. A LOVELY NATIVITY SCENE. ★
3. SERIES 1480 CIRCA 1909. THE
CHRIST CHILD CARRYING A
CHRISTMAS TREE. ★

1. UNITED ART. SANTA WITH APPLIED SOCK ON
CARD. THIS MAY HAVE HAD SOME TYPE OF SWEET
INSERTED. ★★   2. NO. 3151134. SANTA AND AN
ANGEL DELIVER GIFTS TOGETHER. ★★★
3. LANGSDORF SILK SUITED SANTA ON A ROCKING
HORSE. ★★★

A merry Christmas

1. PRINTED IN GERMANY. THIS IS OBVIOUSLY
A SANTA WHO IS USED TO WALKING LONG DIS-
TANCES RATHER QUICKLY, AND IS DRESSED FOR IT.
HIS STAFF WITH HOLLY TOP WAS FOR WALKING
AND PROTECTION. ★★   2. ASB NO. 185. A BERLIN
PUBLISHER. SANTA IS NOT ONLY THE GIFT GIVER
BUT HE ALSO PLAYS THE PART OF EDUCATOR IN
THIS GOLD-ENHANCED CARD. ★★

A Merry Christmas

1. INTERNATIONAL ART. IN FRONT OF AN INN
CALLED THE MISTLETOE BOUGH A CAVALIER
KISSES A PRETTY GIRL WHILE CHILDREN THROW
SNOWBALLS AND A WOMAN LOOKS ON RATHER
SHOCKED AT SUCH SCANDALOUS CONDUCT. ★
2. STECKER PUBLISHING 338 B. THE OPEN DOOR IS
A GLIMPSE INTO ANOTHER WORLD, THE WORLD OF
CHRISTMAS. THE CHILD AT PLAY WITH HIS NEW
CHRISTMAS TOYS IS USING THE PLAY WORLD OF
TOYS TO GLIMPSE INTO THE WORLD OF ADULTS. ★

Bibliography

Anderson, Allan and Tomlinson, Betty. *Greetings From Canada*. Macmillan of Canada, 1978.

Apkarian-Russell, Pamela E. *Collectible Halloween*. Schiffer Publishing, 1997.

Apkarian-Russell, Pamela E. *Halloween: Collectible Decorations and Games*. Schiffer Publishing, 2000.

Apkarian-Russell, Pamela E. *More Halloween Collectibles*. Schiffer Publishing, 1998.

Apkarian-Russell, Pamela E. *The Tastes & Smells of Halloween*. Trick or Treat Trader Publication, 2000.

Dale, Rodney. *Louis Wain The Man Who Drew Cats*. Chris Beetles Publishing, 2000.

Dell'Aquila, Antonio and Pia. *Raphael Kirchner & His Postcards*. Mario Adda Editore Bari, Italy.

Duval, William with Monahan, Valerie. *Collecting Postcards*. Blandford Press, 1978.

Fanelli, Giovanni and Godoli, Envio. *Art Nouveau Postcards*. Patrick Hawkey & Co Ltd., London, 1987.

Gordon, Leslie. *Green Magic*. Viking Press, 1977.

Gutzman, W.L. *The Canadian Patriotic Post Card Handbook 1904–1914*. Unitrade Press, 1985.

Jacob, Dorothy. *A Witches Guide to Gardening*. Taplinger Publishing, 1965.

James, Peter. *Russian Art on Old Postcards*. St. Andrews Press, United Kingdom, 1999.

Kallir, Jane. *Viennese Design and the Wiener Werkstatte*. Thames & Hudson, 1986.

Klamkin, Marian. *Picture Postcards*. Dodd, Mead & Co., 1974.

Kyrou, Ado. *L'Age D'Or De La Carte Postale*. Andre Balland, Paris, 1966.

Mashburn, J.L. *The Postcard Price Guide*. Colonial House Production, 1992.

Monahan, Valerie. *The American Postcard Collector's Guide*. Blandford Press, United Kingdom, 1981.

Morrison, James S. *A Vintage View of Christmas Past*. Shuman/Heritage Press, 1995.

Neudin, Gerard. *Les Meilleures Cartes Postales D' Illustrateurs*. 1991.

Nicholson, Susan Brown. *The Encyclopedia of Antique Postcards*. Wallace Homestead Books, 1994.

Ouellette, William. *Fantasy Postcard*. Doubleday & Co., 1975.

Parkin, Michael. *Louis Wain's Cats*. Thames & Hudson, 1983.

Richardson Alan. *Spirits of the Stones*. Virgin, 2000.

Robinson, Gertrude Ina. *Floral Fairies the Mistletoe's Pranks*. Floral Fairies Publishing Co., 1913.

Russell, C. J. and The Halloween Queen. *Halloween Checklist*. Whitney, 1988.

Ryan, Dorothy. *Picture Postcards in the United States, 1893–1918*. Clarkson N. Potter, Inc., 1982.

Saleh, Nouhad A. *Guide to Artist's Signatures & Monograms on Postcards*. Minerva Press, 1993.

Smith, J.H.D., editor. *The Picture Postcards of Raphael Tuck & Sons*. IPM, 2000.

Smith, J.H.D. *Picture Postcard Values* Vol. 1–27 1974–2001. IPM Publishing, United Kingdom, 2001.

Staff, Frank. *The Picture Postcard & Its Origins*. Frederick A. Praeger, Publishers, 1966.

Ternon, Yves and Kebebdjian, J.C. *Armenie 1900*. Editions Astrid, 1979.

Westwood, Peter J. *The Deltiology of Robert Burns*. Creedon Publications, 1994.

Subscription trade journals:

Picture Postcard Monthly Magazine (and)
Picture Postcard Annual Reflections of a Bygone Age
15 Debdale Lane
Kaywort, Nottingham NG12 5HT
United Kingdom

Barrs News (weekly)
70 South 6th St.
Lansing, IA 52151-0310

Postcard Collector (monthly)
Krause Publications
700 East State St.
Iola, WI 54945-9984

Trick or Treat Trader (quarterly)
PO Box 499
Winchester, NH 03470

Ephemera News Quarterly of the Ephemera Society of America
PO Box 95
Cazenovia, NY 13035-0095

Museums:

Image File A Journal from the Curt Teich Postcard Archives
Lake County Discovery Museum
Route 176 & Fairfield Road
Wauconda, IL 60084

National Christmas Center Museum
3427 Lincoln Highway
Paradise, PA 17562